SOLDIERS AND SAILORS
OF THE EASTERS SHORE OF VIRGINIA
IN THE REVOLUTIONARY WAR

Stratton Nottingham

HERITAGE BOOKS
2008

HERITAGE BOOKS
AN IMPRINT OF HERITAGE BOOKS, INC.

Books, CDs, and more—Worldwide

For our listing of thousands of titles see our website
at
www.HeritageBooks.com

Published 2008 by
HERITAGE BOOKS, INC.
Publishing Division
100 Railroad Ave. #104
Westminster, Maryland 21157

Other books by the author:

Accomack Tithables, 1663-1695
REVOLUTIONARY SOLDIERS AND SAILORS FROM LANCASTER COUNTY, VIRGINIA
Marriage License Bonds of Northumberland County, Virginia: From 1783 to 1850
Virginia Land Causes: Lancaster County, 1795 - 1848 and Northampton County, 1731 -1868
Wills and Administrations of Accomack, 1663-1800
Accomack (Virginia) Land Causes, 1728-1825
Accomack County, Virginia Certificates and Rights 1663-1709, and Tithables 1663-1695
CD: Accomack, Virginia Land Causes, 1728-1825
CD: Virginia Land Causes: Lancaster County, 1795-1848; Northampton County, 1731-1868

International Standard Book Numbers
Paperbound: 978-1-58549-386-9
Clothbound: 978-0-7884-7101-8

CONTENTS

Introduction v

Accomack County 1

Northampton County 81

Index 115

INTRODUCTION

Stratton Nottingham of Onancock, Virginia, compiled county court records of Accomack and Northampton Counties which related to service in the Revolutionary War. His book, *Revolutionary Soldiers and Sailors from Accomack County, Virginia*, contained "recommendations by the Court of persons suitable for officers of the County Militia; the records of commissions from the Governor, and of qualification by the person appointed." As he states in his introduction, "This Court material also includes the declarations of applicants for pension, which often contains much information, not only as to the family of the applicant, but also contemporary testimony as to location of troops, changes in regimental or general officers, and other military information."

Mr. Nottingham notes that this material supplements the data available in the Virgina State Library and Archives and we would add, the National Archives.

His work dealing with Northampton County Revolutionary War records also included data of the War of 1812 which we have omitted here. The book was entitled, *Revolutionary Soldiers and Sailors from Northampton County, Virginia. Muster Rolls and Pay Rolls of the Twenty-Seventh Regiment of Virginia Militia, Northampton County 1812.* The records of the Revolutionary War of Northampton County also contain recommendations, appointments of commissioned officers, claims and references to pension applications revealing family relationships.

For reasons of clarity and economy, Mr. Nottingham's works have been edited (and a few errors corrected). In his original work he copied the court records ver batim, including the repetitious language required by the court. We have eliminated much of this repetition. In reading the statement of family relationships, realize that these are judgments rendered by the court which based its decision on the applicant's statements and other evidence.

Based on the statement of the veterans' applications the following can be derived.

The Eastern Shore of Virginia was very much exposed to the enemy. Frequent alarms were given and the militia was often compelled to turn out to defend the two counties. The militia was frequently called out to keep guard and was in service a considerable portion of the time. The companies were sometimes divided and portions of them performed service alternately, in keeping guard and attending alarms. The major goal of the militia was to prevent the enemy from obtaining supplies, plundering the country and burning the houses. The militia never marched out of either county except some of the units which were sent north to subdue the tories in Somerset County, Maryland.

Accomack County

An element of the Virginia Line, the Ninth Virginia Regiment served for a while in Accomack County before being called north.

From the veterans' statements the following was revealed about the militia organization of Accomack County:

County Lieutenant - George Corbin who resigned and was replaced by John Cropper.

2nd Regt Va. Militia - commanded by Col. Southy Simpson until his death and then by Col. George Corbin, later Cropper. One of the majors was Major Spiers.

The following company captains of the militia were mentioned by the veterans in their applications in later years. The description of the deployment of each company is a compilation of the veterans' statements.

Thomas Bayly's company - nothing specific noted.

Thomas Copes' company - They performed guard duty at the barracks near a wind mill on George Parker's land. At one time the company was marched to Salisbury by Col. Simpson to suppress the tories. Members of the company kept guard at Col. Cropper's barracks or blockhouse and other places. They were stationed mostly on Folly Creek, East Point on Onancock and on Wachapreague.

Thomas Marshall's company - They were stationed at a fort at

Musqueto Point on the Pocomoke River for several weeks where a guard was kept. One-half of the company was stationed at Col. Corbin's landing and the other half at the fort. Some were on guard at Wallops Island for several weeks; they also performed duty of several weeks on Onancock Creek. They also stood guard at Wisherts Landing. They were on guard 1 day to several weeks, and responding to alarms and marching to various parts of the county much of the time. The company also went to Salisbury, Maryland to subdue the tories.

William Polk's company - They performed duty at Upshur's Point, at Col. Parramore's Landing and at Metomkin Inlet; they were also stationed on Watchapreague near the sea coast.

Robert Coleburn's company - The company was stationed most of the time on Wachapreague and Metomkin Creeks.

Nathan Bell's company - They performed duty at Metomkin Inlet and other places in the county.

Richard Savage's company - At one time they went to Hog Island and continued there 10 months without interruption in constant service and later were removed to the mainland and still continued service.

Jesse Dickerson's company - This unit kept guard on Pocomoke River at Chincoteague and at Col. Cropper's barracks; they also kept guard at Houldings Creek and other places on the sea and bay side.

Americus Scarborough's company - This company was attached to Col. William Parramore's Regiment according to one of the veterans; they were stationed mostly on Craddock and Occohannock Creeks.

Richard Justice's company - They kept guard at Assawoman Creek and other places, they were called on guard at a place called the Block House.

John Moore's company - This unit kept guard on Folly Creek and at a fort called the Block House on Pocomoke River, also Assawoman and other places and on Hog Island where they had an engagement with several barges of the enemy and took one of their boats.

Northampton County

Little was revealed about the militia organization of Northampton County. James Carter mentioned serving in a garrison company at a fort on Kings Creek which was under the command of Captain William Davenport.

Regulars

Citizens of the Eastern Shore of Virginia enlisted in various elements of the Virginia Line. Many served as members of the Ninth Regiment which at one point in time was stationed in Accomack County at Pungoteague, before being deployed to the north into Pennsylvania and New Jersey. During the War the regiment was under the command of Col. Levin Joynes, Col. John Cropper, in that order. Some members participated in the Battle of Germantown.

Abbreviations:

admin. - administration
admr. - administrator
co. - county
dau(s). - daughter(s)
lieut. - lieutenant
regt. - regiment
rep. - representative(s)
S.N. - a reference to the original compiler, Stratton Nottingham

F. Edward Wright
Westminster, Maryland
1995

ACCOMACK COUNTY

ORDERS 1774 - 1777

"At the Court House in the County of Accomack on Tuesday the 30 day of July, 1777. The Honourable the Continental Congress having Declared the thirteen United States of America Free and Independent and the Convention of this Colony of Virginia having founded a new Plan of Government in the Name of the CommonWealth and passed an Ordinance wherein all the Magistrates Named in the last Commission of the Peace for this County under Our late King are Continued on their Qualifying themselves according to the Direction of the said Ordinance. William Williams and George Stewart Gent., two Persons Named in the said late Commission Administered the Oath prescribed in the said Ordinance to Tully Robinson Wise, Gentleman, the first Person Presented Named in the said Commission And then the said Tully Robinson Wise Administered the said Oath to William Selby, William Williams, John Smith, Thomas Teackle, George Stewart, Thomas Bayly and William Parramore, Gentlemen. Seven other Persons named in the said Late Commission." p. 448

[Militia appointments]

Edmund Scarburgh, appointed Captain of a company of the Militia in this county; Thomas Parramore, is appointed lieut. 1 June 1777. p. 179.
Thomas Hall, appointed County Lieut.
Thomas Bayly, appointed Lieut. Colonel. 25 April 1775. p. 339.
Covington Corbin, appointed Colonel. 27 June 1775. p. 363.

ORDERS 1777 - 1780

George Poulson recommended as Ensign in the militia. 29 July 1777.
Recommended: Joseph Matthews, 1st lieut.; Southy White, 2nd lieut.; George Marshall, 2nd lieut.; Thomas Copes, 2nd lieut. and William Snead, captain.
Recommended: William Selby, lieut. colonel, Selby Simpson, major to 1st Battalion and Clement Parker as Colonel; William Parramore as Lieut. Colonel and Henry Custis as major of the 2nd Battalion. 29 July 1777. p. 12.
Recommended: Charles Marshall, captain; William Parker, capt.; Robinson Custis, lieut.; Thomas Slocumb, lieut.; Southy Copes, lieut.; Ismael Andrews, lieut.; Francis Savage, lieut.; Zerobabel Watson, lieut.; Thomas Young, lieut.; Joseph Kelly, lieut.; Thomas Lillistone, ensign; Stephen Marshall, ensign; and George Truet Taylor, ensign.

Commissioned as officers in the milita of this county: William Selby, lieut. col.; Selby Simpson, major of the 1st Battalion; Clement Parker, col. and Henry Custis, major of the 2nd Battalion of the militia. 30 July 1777. p. 17.

Commissioned of officers in the militia of this county: William Parker, Solomon Smith, Joseph Kelly, George Justice, George Truet Taylor, Ismael Andrews, Francis Savage, Thomas Young, Zerrobabel Watson; John Dix and Southy Copes. 30 July 1777. p. 18.

Recommended; Robert Coleburn, capt.; George Ashby, 1st lieut.; George Garrison, 2nd lieut. and John Custis, ensign. 26 Aug 1777. p. 23.

Recommended: Reuben Joynes, 2nd lieut.; Michael Bonewell, ensign; Joseph Staten, 1st lieut.; Elijah Fitzgerald; Capt. Cornelious Ironmonger, 1st lieut.; Smith Millener, 2nd lieut.; Benjn. Peck, ensign; John Walker, capt.; Levin Window, capt.; Thomas Russel, lieut.; Andrew Russel, ensign. 26 Aug 1777. p. 23.

Qualified: Andrew Russell, ensign; Thomas Russel, lieut.; Joseph Staten, lieut.; Robert Coleburn, capt.; George Garrison, lieut.; Michael Bonewell, ensign; Elijah Fitzgerald, capt.; Cornelius Ironmonger, lieut.; Peter Savage, ensign. 26 Aug 1777. p. 24.

Recommended: Parker Barns, capt.; Abel West, lieut.; Thomas Sandford, lieut.; Solomon Johnson, ensign. 31 Sept 1777. p. 28.

Qualified: Thomas Copes, capt.; Parker Barns, lieut.; Abel West, lieut.; Thomas Sandford, lieut.; Elijah Stokely, lieut.; Solomon Johnson, ensign. 31 Sept 1777. p. 29.

Recommended: Thomas Burton, ensign in the room of John Custis who refused; John West, son of Jonathan West, lieut.; both qualified. 1 Oct 1777. p. 30.

Recommended and qualified: Major Colony, lieut.; Isaac Lewis, capt.; John Turnal, lieut.; Zerobabel Rodgers as capt. in room of Edward Revel, (resigned); John Riley as lieut. in room of Ramond Riley; John Custis (B.S.) as capt. in room of William Riley. 25 Nov 1777. pp. 38-39.

Recommended: Zorobabel Rodgers and John Custis, captains - qualified.

Recommended: Tully Wise, 2d lieut.

Esther Bunting, wife of Ritchie Bunting, a poor soldier now in the service of the Continental States allowed 12/6 pr month from 1 June last to this time for her support and maintenance.

Agnes Hogshire, wife of Robt. Hogshire, a poor soldier now in service, allowed 30/ pr month from 5 May last to this time for the support of herself and her three children.

Comfort Bloxom, widow of Charles Bloxom, a poor soldier, allowed 12/6 per month from middle of June last to middle of Sept for support of herself and child. 26 Nov 1777. p. 41.

Qualified: John Riley, lieut.

Recommended and qualified: William Vessels, ensign. 26 Nov 1777. p. 43.

Amy Belote, widow of William Belote, dec'd., late a soldier in the Continental Army allowed 12/6 pr month for support and maintenance of herself and children.

Metty McCollester, widow of Daniel McCollester, late a soldier in the Continental Army, allowed 12/6 pr month for support and maintenance of herself and three children. 24 Feb 1778. p. 57.

Reuben Joynes, qualified as lieut. of the militia. 27 May 1778. p. 88.

Elizabeth Mendom, widow of Robert Mendom, late a soldier in the Continental Army, allowed 12/6 pr month from March 1777 (being the time her husband died) to this date - for support and maintenance of herself and children. 27 May 1778. p. 89.

Patience Ketslaugh, widow of Jacob Ketslaugh, a poor soldier who died in the service of the Continental States, allowed £3 pr month for support of herself and two children from 6 May 1777 to this date. 27 Jan 1779. p. 298.

Susannah Howard, widow of Nehemiah Howard, a poor soldier who died in the service of the Continental States, allowed £3 pr month for the support of herself and two children from 1 Apr 1777 to this date. 23 Feb 1779.

Jacob Phillips allowed 30 shillings pr month for support of a dau. of William Turnal, a poor soldier who died in the service of the Continental States from 25 Feb 1777 to this date. 27 Jan 1779. p. 299.

Bridget Cobb, widow of Stratton Cobb, a poor soldier who died in the service of the Continental State, allowed £4.10 pr month for support of herself and three children, from 1 March 1778 to this date. 23 Feb 1779. p. 320.

Sarah Jones, wife of John Jones, a poor soldier, now in the service of the Continental States, allowed £3 pr month from 1 Jan 1779 to this date for support of herself and two children.

Nanny Simpson, widow of Salathiel Simpson, a poor soldier who died in the said service, from July 1777 to this date. 23 Feb 1779. p. 324.

Priscilla Tignah allowed £30 from Oct 1777 till March 1779 for support of herself and three children.

Jessee Evans allowed £24 for keeping a poor soldier's orphan for 12 months. 30 March 1779. p. 328.

Scarbrough Clerk, widow of George Clerk, a poor soldier who died in the service, allowed £3 pr month from 1 Jan 1779 to this date for her maintenance and support. 27 Apr 1779. p. 332.

Molly Copes, widow of Solomon Copes, a poor soldier who died in the service, allowed £3 pr month from 28 Jan 1778 to this date for her support. 28 Apr 1779. p. 337.

Parker Barnes recommended capt. of a company in the room of John Pettigrew. Also William Fisher as lieut. to same company. Also George Bundick as ensign in the room of Andrew Russell. 25 May 1779. p. 371.

Recommended: William Selby, col. for the Upper Battalion; Selby Simpson, lieut. Col. for the same and William Young, major.; Richard Justice, capt. to William Young's company; Solomon Reid 1st lieut. to Capt. Rodger's company and James Twiford, son of John, ensign; Americus Scarburgh, capt. to the company formerly Lecatte's; Caleb Aimes, lieut. and Elisha Mears, ensign. 29 Sept 1779. p. 431.

ORDERS 1780 - 1783

John Custis recommended capt. 30 Aug 1780. p. 86.

George Stewart and Charles Bagwell allowed £1500 each for their services as Commissioners for purchasing provisions and acting under instructions from the Governour. 29 March 1781. p. 142.

John Cropper recommended as county lieut. in the room of George Corbin (resigned from bodily infirmities).

Recommended: Joseph Staten as before as capt. in the room of William Downing (resigned); John Nicholson, ensign in the said company; Johannis Watson as capt. in the room of William Parker (resigned). 28 March 1781. p. 142.

Recommendation of Johannes Watson as capt. in the room of William Parker (resigned) is rescinded and Southy Copes recommended in his room. 25 Apr 1781. p. 149.

Recommended: Southy Bull, lieut. in Capt. Garret's Company of Militia. 29 May 1781. p. 154.

Recommended: William Drummond, lieut. in the room of Thomas Slocomb; Garret Topping as capt. in the room of John Riley Parker. 26 June 1781. p. 157.

Recommended: William Parramore, col. in the room of Clement Parker (resigned); Henry Custis, lieut. col. of the militia in the room of William Parramore; Richard Savage, major in the room of Henry Custis; Nathaniel Bell, capt. in the room of Richard Savage. 30 Apr 1782. p. 217.

Mary Kelly, wife of William Kelly, a soldier in the Continental Army, allowed 5 bushels of corn for her support and maintenance. Elizabeth Mardrick, wife of Elisha Mardrick, allowed 6 bushels of corn. Elizabeth Benston, wife of George Benston, allowed 10 bushels of corn. 28 May 1782. p. 226.

Naomi Fisher, wife of Thomas Fisher, soldier in the Army allowed 3 barrels of corn and 150 weight of pork for the support and maintenance of herself and 3 small children. Also Elizabeth Colony, wife of George Colony, a soldier, and her 2 children, allowed 2 barrels of corn and 100 weight of pork. Also Catherine Topping, wife of Major Topping, a soldier, and 1 child, allowed 1 barrel of corn and 50 weight of pork. Also Elizabeth Mardrick, widow of Elisha Mardrick, a soldier who died in the service, and her 3 children, allowed 3 barrels of corn and 150 weight or pork. 31 Jan 1783. p. 433.

ORDERS 1783 - 1784

Richard Drummond, Junr. is allowed for finding himself rations for 2 months on duty in the militia, a light horse. Garret Topping is allowed £3.13.0 for services performed in the Militia. William Polk is allowed for repairing arms for the Militia 13 shillings. Arthur Teackle is allowed £1.8.0 for services performed for the State and £45 for the Continent. 26 Nov 1783. p. 166.

Charles Snead who had served in the Continental Army as a captain has lost his certificate for his arrears of pay and depreciation and entered into recognizance with Major Smith Snead, his security in the sum of £15. 29 Apr 1784. p. 295.

Phillip Toddison has lost his certificate and discharge from Major Edmunds of the Southern Army for 18 months' service as a foot soldier and this day entered into recognizance together with John Cropper, his security in the sum of £72. 30 Apr 1784. p. 302.

George Arbuckle presented an account against the State amounting to £20.3.3 for his pay and rations as Commissary of Issues under Major John Poulson from 1 Jan 1781 until last day of Apr following, which is ordered "certified and transmitted." 28 July 1784. p. 379.

George Hall made oath that he entered on board the Henry Galley formerly stationed in this county on 16 March 1777 and was discharged therefrom on 24 March 1780, and that he had lost his discharge from Capt. Barron and thereupon entered into bond with John Joynes his security in the sum of £60. 26 July 1785. p. 354.

ORDERS 1787 - 1790

James Rodgers allowed £12 yearly in consequence of his being disabled in the Service. The Sheriff is to pay him two years pension at the above rate as he is allowed in the said certificate from 1 Jan 1786. Certificate reads that James Rodgers, aged about 29 years, a private in the 9th Va. Regt. and his pay was at the rate of £24 per annum was disabled in the Service of the United States by a wound received in his right leg. Allowed £12 yearly to commence from 1 Jan 1786. Signed Beverly Randolph [on] 21 May 1787. 27 Feb 1788. p. 112.

ORDERS 1796 - 1798

Comfort Bloxom, widow of Charles alias Stewart Bloxom, who died a private in the 9th Va. Regt. ... ought to be continued on the pension list. 1 Nov 1796. p. 149.

Margaret Groten, widow of John Groten, who died a private in the 9th Va. Regt. ... ought to be continued on the pension list. 1 Nov 1796. p. 148.

ORDERS 1804 - 1805

Agnes Hogshire, late a pensioner of this State, died 1 Oct last. 25 Nov 1805. p. 446.

John Drummond is certified as heir at law of James Drummond who was a lieut. in the 9th Regiment on Continental Establishment and died in the American Army during the Revolutionary War. 7 May 1807. p. 326.

To be certified to the register of the land office of this Commonwealth that -

Esther Holland is the representative of Major Johnson, a soldier in the Rev. War.

Levin Hyslop representative of Abner Hyslop.

Anne McGee representative of Archibald McGee.

Isaac Dix representative of Thomas Metcalf and Walter Metcalf.

Euphamy Watson representative of Caleb Parker.

Patience Prescott representative of Thomas Prescott.

Rachel and Nany Turlington representatives of Jacob Turlington.

Daniel Richison representative of Zerobabel, Charles and William Richison.

James Ailworth representative of James Ailworth.

William Andrews representative of William Andrews, Sergt.
Micajah Annis representative of James Annis.
Thomas Ayres is representative of Francis Ayres.
Ezeniah Bloxom representative of Ezekiel Bloxom (of William).
William Bloxom representative of Ezekiel Bloxom.
Thomas Kelly representative of Thomas Bloxom, Woodman Bloxom, Levi
    Bloxom and John Bloxom.
Anora Lurton and John Lurton representatives of Richard Bunting.
John Bunting, John Watson and Seymour Bunting representatives of
    Smith Bunting.
Joseph Burton representative of Benjamin Burton.
Sophia Williams and John Williams representatives of William Crippen.
William Cobb and Susa Cobb representatives of Stratton Cobb.
William Damerell representative of Jacob Damerell.
Elizabeth Dickison representative of Edw. Dickison.
Tabitha Simpson representative of Severn Darby.
Thomas Evans representative of Thomas Evans.
George Christopher and George Wilson representatives of John Fisher
    and Bartho: Fisher.
Levin Gray representative of Thomas Gray.
William Hinman representative of Elijah Hinman.
Jacob Kelly representative of John Harman, Levin Harman and Ezekiel
    Harman.
John Hutchinson representative of John Huchison.
William Hogshire representative of Robert Hogshire.
James Thornton representative of Henry Jones.
John Lurton representative of William Lurton and Levin Lurton.
Elijah Lilliston representative of John Lilliston.
Edward Martin representative of James Martin.
Stephen Moon (Moor?) representative of Levi Moon.
Smith Milliner representative of Henry Milliner, Sergt.
James Nelson representative of Robert Nelson, Sergt.
John Nock representative of William Nock.
Richard Parker representative of Levin Parker.
Susa Potter representative of John Potter.
Benjamin Phillips representative of Charles Phillips and Elijah Phillips.
John Ross representative of Elijah Ross.
Tabitha Simpson representative of Elisha Simpson.
Hancock Simpson representative of Sacker Scott.
John Read representative of Henry Window.
Cornelius Watkinson representative of Levin Watkinson.

Isaac Whaley representative of William Whaly.
Sophia Williams and John Williams representatives of John Williams.
John Madrick representative of Elisha Madrick.
Henry Sterling representative of Richard Sterling and William Sterling.
   2 Sept 1807. p. 379 et seq.

William Joynes representative of Reuben Joynes, dec'd., a lieut. in the
   Rev. War.
Nancy Stevens representative of Elijah Hickman, dec'd., and Ezekiel
   Hickman, dec'd., soldiers.
Majors Andrews representative of William Andrews.
Margaret Lingo representative of Jedediah White.
Rachel Richards representative of John Richards, William Richards and
   Preeson Richards.
John Taylor representative of George Philby.
Jonathan Bunting representative of Holloway Bunting and Coventon
   Evans.
Patience Bunting representative of Sacker Bunting.
Smith Melson representative of John Carss.
James Cheshire representative of John Cheshire.
28 Oct 1807. p. 418.

ORDERS 1807 - 1809
Margaret Bunting is the only child and heiress of William Black Bunting,
dec'd., an officer in the American Army during the Rev. War.
Betty Case is only heir of William Case and John Case, soldiers.
John Hart is only heir of John Hart, a soldier.
Margaret Lingo of Robinson Lingo; William Onions of Selby Onions;
Priscilla Harman of Zerobabel Harman; Anthony Mathews of Thomas
Bennett; Agness Lingo of Thomas Lingo; Jesse Gladding of John
Delastatious; Robert Broadwater of Caleb Broadwater, and Peggy Mears
of Francis Downing and William R. Finney of John Finney, all soldiers in
the American Army in the Rev. War. 1 June 1808. p. 111.

ORDERS 1809 - 1811
Obed Watson, Letitia Watson, heirs of Americus Watson and Jesse
Watson are the only heirs and representative of David Watson, a soldier
in the American Army in the Rev. War. 25 Sept 1809. p. 7.
Elizabeth Walker, Ann Harman, Sally Walker, Henry Walker, James
Walker and John S. Walker are devisees of John Walker, an ensign in the

Army of the United States in the Rev. War. Eliza. Walker, one of the children being dead without issue. Also Sally Evans representative of Jesse Evans, a fifer in the Rev. War. 25 Sept 1809. p. 9.

John Gladding is the only heir and representative of John Gladding, and William Thornman is the heir of William Thornman, soldiers in the American Army in the Rev. War. 31 Oct 1809. p. 20.

Samuel Ashby, Ezekiel Ashby and Elizabeth Ashby, James Ashby, George Ashby, Catherine Ashby, Molly Beach, Catherine Beach, James Ashby, William Savage, Sally Jacob, John Savage, Eliza. Savage, Rowland Savage and Mary Drummond are the heirs of David Ashby, a soldier in the 9th Va. Regt. upon Continental Establishment during the Rev. War. 29 Jan 1810. p. 58.

Ann Shipherd is the only heir of Major Shiphard who was only heir of Solomon Shipherd, a soldier in the Rev. War. 29 Jan 1810. p. 59.

Nehemiah Stockly, Ann B. Stockly, Charles T. Stockly, Harriot Stockly, Ayres Stockly and Elizabeth, wife of Thompson Holmes are the children and heirs of Charles Stockly, late of this county, dec'd. 29 Mar 1810. p. 101.

Elizabeth Lewis, wife of Custis Lewis, William S. Drummond, Ann T. Drummond, Richard H. Drummond and Catherine S. Drummond are the only children and heirs of William Drummond dec'd., a soldier of the 9th Va. Regt. during the Rev. War. 30 July 1810. p. 198.

Susanna Wyatt, Molly Wyatt, Thomas Wyatt, Patty Wyatt and Molly Churn are the only heirs of Thomas Wyatt, a soldier in the 9th Va. Regt. on Continental Establishment during the American Rev. War.

Kendall Hyslop is the only heir to Smith Hyslop, a soldier in the 9th Va. Regt. on Continental Establishment during the American Rev. War. 25 Mar 1811. p. 285.

Peggy Meers is the only heir of Francis Downing, a soldier in the 9th Va. Regt. upon Continental Establishment during the Rev. War. 25 Mar 1811. p. 286.

James Watkinson is brother and only heir of William Watkinson, dec'd., a soldier in the 9th Virginia on Continental Establishment during the Rev. War. 29 July 1811. p. 372.

Betsy Guy, wife of George Guy is the only heir of Robert Martin, a soldier in the 9th Va. Regt. during the Rev. War. 30 Sept 1811. p. 398.

Peggy Churn, wife of William Churn, is only heir of Jacob Kestlar, a soldier in the 9th Va. Regt. on Continental Establishment during the Rev. War. 30 Sept 1811. p. 398.

Major Lecatte, Betsy Lecatte, James Hornsby, John Downing, Molly Turner, Betsy Brown, Peggy Brittingham, Babel Heath, Edmund Heath and James Heath are the only heirs of Ezekiel Hornsby, a soldier in the 9th Va. Regt. on Continental Establishment in the Rev. War. The same persons are the only heirs of Levi Hornsby, 9th Va. Regt., on Continental Establishment in the Rev. War. 28 Oct 1811. p. 402.

ORDERS 1812 - 1814
Leah Mears, wife of Robert; Rachel Tignal, widow of Dennis; Mary Beach, Levin Beach, James Beach and Caty and Peggy Beach, children of Frederick Beach, are the only heirs of John Beach, dec'd., a soldier in the 9th Va. Regt. on Continental Establishment in the Rev. War. 27 Jan 1812. p. 2.

ORDERS 1815 - 1817
William Dix went to sea about 10 years ago; has not since been heard from and is presumed dead. William Dix, Tabitha Watson, wife of Jno. Watson, Peggy Bonwell, wife of Jesse Bonwell, and Hessey Sparrow, wife of John Sparrow, are the only heirs and representative of said William Dix, a sergeant who served 3 years in the 9th Va. Regt. during the Rev. War. 26 May 1815. p. 41.

ORDERS 1817 - 1819
Margaret Core, wife of William Core, is the only heir at law of William Black Bunting, dec'd., who was an ensign in the American Army in the Rev. War and was native of this county, a resident of this county at the time of his death. 2 Apr 1818. p. 141.

ORDERS 1819 - 1822
John Beasley, on whose estate Thomas R. Joynes hath this day qualified as admr., died 21st instant. He is the same soldier in the Rev. War to whom a pension was granted under the late act of Congress. 21 Aug 1819. p. 7.

William Bunting, on whose estate William Nock this day qualified as admr., is the same soldier in the 11th Va. Regt. in the Rev. War to whom a pension was granted under the act of Congress passed 18 March 1818, and who died 8th of this month, and who resided in Accomack Co. 30 March 1820. p. 104.

Declaration of Thomas Moore, age 80. Enlisted under Capt. Thomas Davis of 9th Va. Regt. on Continental Establishment. The company was later commanded by Capt. Smith Snead. He served the two years and a pension was granted under act of 1818, #11620; applied 5 March 1819. His family consists of wife Tabitha, age 60. 1 Aug 1820. p. 163.

Declaration of William Taylor, age 60. Enlisted in 11th Va. Regt. on Continental Establishment, commanded by Col. Arthur Campbell in a company commanded by Capt. William Davenport; he served 18 months and received pension under act of 1818, certificate #9947; applied 20 Oct 1818. His family consists of wife age 40 and 3 daus.; eldest is Savea age 18; 2nd is Sarah age 12; and youngest is Julia Ann age 8. 1 Aug 1820. p. 164.

Declaration of Zadock Bayly, age 59. Enlisted to serve for duration of war in the company commanded by Capt. Thomas Parker in 11th Va. Regt. on Continental Establishment; served til the end of the war; pension granted under act of 1818. He has a female child Ritta 11 years of age to support; he and his dau. live with his son's family. 1 Aug 1820. p. 165.

Declaration of William Lilliston, age 64. Enlisted in a company commanded by Capt. Thomas Snead in the 9th Va. Regt. on Continental Establishment, commanded by Col. Thomas Fleming; served 2 years. A pension was granted under the act of 1818, certificate #6875; he applied 9 July 1818. His family consisted of his wife Elizabeth, age 48 and 3 children: Selby age 13, Leah age 10 and Asa age 7. 1 Aug 1820. p. 166.

Declaration of Solomon Russell, age 64 Nov next. Enlisted in a company commanded by Capt. Thomas Parramore in 9th Va. Regt, on Continental Establishment, commanded by Col. Thomas Flemming; he served 2 years. Pension #4408; applied 9 July 1818 under act of 1818. Has wife Jamima, age 54 and stepson age 14. 1 Aug 1820. p. 166.

Declaration of William Raleigh, age 68. Enlisted in the company of Capt. Thomas Snead, 9th Va. Regt.; served 2 years. Pension #4409; applied 9 July 1818 under act of 1818. Has no family. 1 Aug 1820. p. 167.

Declaration of Solomon Bunting, age 78 on 20 Sept 1820. Enlisted in the company of Capt. John Blair, 9th Va. Regt.; served 18 months. Pension #14093; applied 3 Aug 1818 under act of 1818. Has wife Sarah age 50 and two daus., Peggy age 16 and Sally age 11. 2 Aug 1820. p. 170.

Declaration of Samuel Russell, age 71. Enlisted in company of Capt. Thomas Snead, 9th Va. Regt; served 2 years. Pension 4852; applied 9 July 1818 under act of 1818. Had little girl Lucretia Gray for whose services he gives her victuals and clothes and a hired man named Henry Charnick. 2 Aug 1820. p. 169.

Declaration of Matthias Phillips, age 68. Enlisted in company of Capt. Thomas Parramore, 9th Va. Regt.; served 2 years. Pension 4410; applied 9 July 1818 under act of 1818. Has wife Polly, dau. age 28, and a little girl Rachel Rooks he keeps for her victuals and clothes. 2 Aug 1820. p. 171.

Declaration of Smith Beasley, age 60. Enlisted in company of Capt. Thomas Parker, 11th Va. Regt.; served 18 months. Pension: #6098; applied 9 July 1818 under act of 1818. Has wife Fanny age ca. 60 and son Edmund age 8. 2 Aug 1820. p. 172.

Declaration of Severn Scott, age 66. Enlisted in company of Capt. Thomas Snead, 9th Va. Regt.; served 2 years. Pension: #4850; applied 9 July 1818. Has wife Nancy age 37, son James age 2 years, 6 months, dau. Suckey age 18 months. 2 Aug 1820. p. 173.

Declaration of Jacob Teague, age 63. Enlisted in company of Capt. Thomas Parker, 11th Va. Regt.; served 18 months. Applied for pension on 15 May 1819. Has wife Alicia age 29 and 2 step-children, Arthur Harmon in his 11th year and a step-son age 7. 2 Aug 1820. p. 174.

Declaration of John Charnock, age 64. Enlisted in company of Capt. Thomas Parker, 11th Va. Regt.; served 18 months. Applied for pension on 5 May 1819. Had wife Elizabeth age 58; and two children, Sally age 28 and Rosey age 26; and his wife's sister Peggy Charnock age 40, and her 3 children: Nancy age 18, Molly age 10 and William age 7. 2 Aug 1820. p. 175.

Declaration of George Matthews, age 58. Enlisted in company of Capt. Philip Sansom, 1st Va. Regt.; served 18 months. Pension: #11138; applied 29 Oct 1818. Has wife Esther age 50, two daus.: Mehala age 15 and Rosey age 9, and a son Riley age 7, and a small hired boy Custis Vessells age 16. 29 Aug 1820. p. 186.

Declaration of George Justice, age 73. Enlisted in company of Capt. John Cropper, 9th Va. Regt.; served 2 years. Pension: #4804; applied 29 Oct 1818 under act of 1818. Has no family to support; lives as a boarder with his son. 29 Aug 1820. p. 187.

Declaration of George Lewis, age 48. Enlisted in company of Capt. Thomas Parker, 11th Va. Regt.; served 18 months. Applied for pension 5 May 1819. Has a woman called Betsy Hinman age 26 and her child John age 4, to support. 1 Sept 1819. p. 197.

George Matthews, who was a pensioner of the U.S., died 2 Oct 1820 in this county. He is the same person on whose estate admin. has been granted to Thos. Fletcher. 27 Nov 1820. p. 234.

Declaration of Solomon Parks, age 57. Enlisted in the company of Capt. Thomas Parker, 11th Regt.; served 18 months. Applied for pension on 7 May 1819. Has wife Nancy, dau. Comfort age 18, son Charles age 16 and a son Solomon age 11. 28 March 1821. p. 296.

ORDERS 1822 - 1824

Lucretia Bloxom, formerly Lucretia Watson, dau. of Johannes Watson, who was the captain of the Accomack Galley in the service of the Commonwealth of Virginia in the Rev. War, is dead and Sally Bloxom and Fanny Bloxom are her only children and heirs. 28 Oct 1822. p. 90.

Tabitha Bloxom, formerly Tabitha Watson, dau. of Johannes Watson who was capt. of the Accomack Galley in the service of the Commonwealth of Virginia in the Rev. War, is dead, and Walter Bloxom, Asbury Bloxom and Peggy Bloxom are her only children and heirs. 28 Oct 1822. p. 91.

James J. Teackle and Elizabeth A. P. Scarburgh are the only heirs and representatives of Arthur Teackle, dec'd. 25 Feb 1823. p. 146.

Declaration of Levin Hyslop, age 69. Enlisted June 1775 in a company commanded by Capt. John Blair, 9th Va. Regt.; served until 1788; discharged in the Camp at Valley Forge, Pa. Has a wife Susan age 65. He has an interest in 17 acres held by John Davis in right of his wife Susan Hyslop as dower. 28 July 1823. pp. 234-63.

Declaration of William Andrews, age 63. Enlisted 1777 in the Galley called the Accomack commanded by Capt. William Underhill in a fleet commanded by Commodore Barron; served until 1780 when he was discharged at Chincoteague, Va. Has no family; lives with his sister Rachel Rew's family. 3 June 1824. p. 434.

Declaration of Elcanah Andrews, age 57. Enlisted 1777 in a galley called the Accomack commanded by Capt. William Underhill; served until 1779 when he was discharged at Onancock Town. Has a wife Hetty age 40 and children: Robert age 20, Richard age 11 and Samuel age 8. 3 June 1824. p. 441.

Jacob Teague, dec'd., of whom John G. Joynes is admr., was the same person who was a pensioner of the U.S. for services during Rev. War; he died 4 Aug 1824. 22 Sept 1824. p. 520.

ORDERS 1824 - 1827

Declaration of Arthur Addison, age 61. Enlisted 1780 in the company of Capt. Thomas Parker, in a Virginia regiment at Cumberland Courthouse in the Army of the U.S. under Col. Quebecca or Febecca; he served until the end of the Rev. War; discharged at Bedford Courthouse, Va., by Capt. Nathan Read of the Army of the U.S. He has a wife Rosey age 38, dau. Elizabeth age 4, son William age 4 months. 26 Oct 1824. pp. 13-119.

Declaration of Parker Copes, age 63. Enlisted in a company of Capt. Thomas Parker, 11th Va. Regt.; served 18 months. He farms on land provided for him by the bounty of his son in law, William Elliott, Accomack Co. He has wife Margaret, dau. in law Rachel Elliott age 21 and Littleton T. Elliott age 18. 1 March 1825. p. 88. At a later date on 31 March 1825 he said he was discharged at Winchester, Va. Pension: 9642. He did not apply to be continued on the pension list before 1 March 1825 because until 19 Feb 1825 he was in possession of property valued at $240. p. 185.

John B. Walker is the only child and heir of Levin Walker, Capt. in the Rev. War. 26 Apr 1825. p. 140.

ORDERS 1827 - 1829

Peter Parker Copes, soldier in the Rev. War, is insolvent and has been for several years, unable to pay his state and county taxes. 30 July 1827. p. 57.

Declaration of William Kennahorn, age 82. Enlisted Feb 1776 in Accomack Co. in the company of Capt. Levin Joynes; served for 2 years; discharged at Valley Forge, Pa. Pension granted under acts of 1818 and 1820. Has wife Delany, age upwards of 50. 28 Apr 1829. p. 515.

Spencer Kellam, age 69. Drafted Accomack Co. Oct 1781 in the company of Capt. Thomas Parker; served for 18 months; discharged at Drummondtown, Accomack Co. He was able to support himself until recently when almost all his property was lost in a storm on the Chesapeake Bay. Has a wife Margaret, age near 70. 28 Apr 1829. p. 517. On 27 July 1829 Spencer Kellam declared that on 18 March 1818 he owned a small shallop and had then two sons with him by which he was enabled by trading in the Chesapeake Bay to support his family. Since then one son has died and the other attaining the age of 21, has left him. Nevertheless he continued to run his shallop and obtain a scanty living until 4 Aug 1828 when in a squall on the Bay he lost his vessel and nearly all his clothes and tools. p. 83.

ORDERS 1829 - 1832
James Thornton, Sr., age 75. Enlisted Feb 1776 in Virginia in the company of Capt. Thomas Snead in the regiment under Col. Matthews; discharged ca. Feb 1778 at Valley Forge. 19 Dec 1829. p. 51.

John R. Savage, Burlington, NJ, Margaret I., wife of Hyacinthe Desire Landy, all of Burlington Co., NJ, and Anne, wife of Alexis De La Folie of the city of Paris, France, are the only heirs of John Savage, dec'd., who was a brother of Nathaniel L. Savage, late a lieut. of cavalry in the Virginia State Line during the Rev. War. 26 July 1820. p. 143.

Euphamia Walston, wife of Samuel Walston, is the only heir of Jenifer Marshall, dec'd., who was a sailing master in the Virginia Navy in the Rev. War.

Caty Hinman, wife of Galen Hinman, is the only heir of Ishmael Andrews, dec'd., who was a lieut. in the Virginia Navy in the Rev. War. 3 Sept 1830. p. 178.

John Murray is the heir at law of David Murray who was a sailing master in the Virginia Navy in the Rev. War. 27 Sept 1830. p. 182.

Smith, John, Southy, Thomas, Tabitha and Anna Maria Milliner and Susanna Hurst, wife of Thomas Hurst, Polly Carey, wife of Samuel S. Carey, Nancy Milliner, devisee of James Milliner, Richard, William, James, Henry, Catherine and Tabitha Drummond, William Dunton and John Dunton are heirs at law of Robert Milliner, dec'd., formerly lieut. in the Virginia Navy in the Rev. War. The said Smith, John, Southy, Thomas, Tabitha and Anna Maria Milliner, James Milliner, Polly Carey, Susanna Hurst being children of Smith Milliner, dec'd., who was the eldest brother of the said Robert Milliner, dec'd., who died before 1 Jan 1787, and the said Richard, William, James, Henry, Catherine and Tabitha Drummond being the children of Catherine Drummond, dec'd., dau. of said Smith Milliner, dec'd., and the said William Dunton and John Dunton being the children of Elizabeth Dunton, dec'd., who was a dau. of said Smith Milliner, dec'd. 27 Sept 1830. p. 187.

James Melson, Levin Lewis, Nancy White, Henry Melson, Cassey Melson, Samuel Melson and Thomas Melson are heirs at law of Levin Melson, dec'd., who was a carpenter in the Virginia Navy in the Rev. War. The said James Melson being son of said Levin Melson; the said Levin Lewis being the only child of Bridget Lewis, dec'd., formerly Bridget Melson, a dau. of said Levin Melson dec'd. and the said Nancy White being the only child of Amey White dec'd. formerly Amer Melson, a dau. of said Levin Melson dec'd. and the said Henry, Cassey, Samuel and Thomas Melson being the only children of Noah Melson dec'd. who was a son of said Levin Melson dec'd. 27 Sept 1830. p. 187.

Leah Cameron formerly Leah Simpson is heir at law of Hancock Simpson dec'd. who was a coxswain in the Virginia Navy in the Rev. War.

Seymour Litchfield is the only heir at law of Thomas Litchfield who was a seaman in the Virginia Navy in the Rev. War. 27 Sept 1830. p. 187.

Littleton S. White and Elizabeth A. White are the only heirs at law of William White formerly of Accomack Co. At the time of his death he was a resident of Worcester Co., Maryland. He was a surgeon's mate in the Virginia Navy in the Rev. War. Said Elizabeth A. White is an infant and Betsey T. White is the widow of the said William White. 26 Oct 1830. p. 192.

William Riley, Thomas Drummond, Richard Drummond, Elizabeth Drummond, Maria Drummond, David Drummond, William T. Drummond,

John W. Downing, Margaret D. James, formerly Margaret D. Downing, George D. Downing, Elizabeth Bloxom, formerly Elizabeth Downing, wife of Samuel Bloxom, Sarah A. Henderson, formerly Sarah Ann Drummond, wife of Samuel Henderson, William M. Riley, Eliza Riley and Ellen G. Dolby, formerly Ellen G. Riley, wife of Nathaniel Dolby and Emily C. Riley, are the heirs at law of William Riley dec'd. formerly a captain in the Virginia State Line in the Rev. War. The said William Riley being a son of the said William Riley dec'd.; the said Richard, Elizabeth, Maria, David and William T. Drummond being children of William R. Drummond dec'd. who together with Thomas Drummond, John W. Downing, Margaret D. James, George D. Downing, Elizabeth Bloxom and Sarah A. Henderson are children of Elizabeth Downing, dec'd., formerly Elizabeth Drummond, formerly Elizabeth Riley who was a dau. of said William Riley dec'd. and the said William M., Eliza and Emily C. Riley and Ellen G. Dolby being the only children of George Riley dec'd. who was a son of said William Riley dec'd. 26 Oct 1830. p. 193.

Betsey Young, Jonathan Young, Thorowgood and Sarah Ann Young, children of William Young, who was a brother of said Betsey and Jonathan Young are the heirs at law of Robert Webb who was formerly in the Virginia Navy in the Rev. War. 30 Nov 1830. p. 205.

Ann Dalby, wife of Lemuel Dalby, and Susan Johnson are the heirs at law of Brandon Dalby dec'd. formerly a seaman in the Virginia Navy in the Rev. War. 30 Nov 1830. p. 205.

John Bailey and John J. Bailey are the heirs at law of Laban Bailey dec'd. who served in the Virginia Navy in the Rev. War. 30 Nov 1830. p. 205.

Sally W. Ames, wife of Thomas Ames, Betsey Hornesby and Ann, wife of Levin Ames and Washington H. Ames, Mary R. Ames, Richard T. Ames and Anathy Ames, infant children of Elizabeth Ames, are the only heirs at law of Levin Bird dec'd. who was formerly in service in the Virginia Navy in the Rev. War. 30 Nov 1830. p. 205.

John Lilliston, James Lilliston, James Hickman, son of Kessey Hickman and Mary Lilliston are the heirs at law of Kessey and Margaret Lilliston, devisees of Sally Cropper, only heir at law of John Cropper dec'd., a carpenter in the Virginia Navy in the Rev. War.

Sabra Case is the only heir at law of Betty Case who was the only heir at law of William Case and John Case, soldiers in the Virginia Line on Continental Establishment during the Rev. War. 30 Nov 1830. p. 205.

William Coard, Charles Boothe, Scarborough Melson, wife of James Melson, Tabitha Snead and William Snead are the heirs at law of Betsey Boothe, who was a devisee and legatee of John Harris, dec'd, a captain in the Virginia Navy in the Rev. War. 30 Nov 1830. p. 205.

Martha Melson, formerly Martha Lumber, Nancy Lee, formerly Nancy Lumber, wife of Andrew Lee, James Lumber, William Lumber, Thomas Lumber and Jane, William, Samuel and Thomas Lumber, children of Samuel Lumber, are the heirs at law of William Lumber dec'd. formerly a gunner in the Virginia Navy during the Rev. War. Martha, Nancy, James, William, Thomas and Samuel, being children of said William Lumber, dec'd. 1 Dec 1830. p. 208.

John W. Snead, now of the state of Ohio, is the only child and heir at law of Robert Snead dec'd. late of this co. and formerly a surgeon in the Virginia Navy during the Rev. War. 1 Dec 1830. p. 208.

Patty, Thomas and Sally Waters are the heirs at law of Isaac Waters who was a boatswains mate in the Virginia Navy in the Rev. War. 27 Dec 1830. p. 215.

John White, Sydney A. White, Henry White, Levin White, Matilda Downing, wife of John W. Downing, Zilpa Devorix, wife of James Devorix, James White, Nancy Cropper, wife of Kendall Cropper, Sally Duncan, wife of Milby Duncan and Edward Scarburgh are the only heirs at law of Jacobus White, formerly a carpenter in the Virginia Navy in the Rev. War. 27 Dec 1830. p. 216.

Sally Beavans, wife of Joshua Beavans, Elizabeth Broadwater, William Broadwater and Rebecca Broadwater, are the only heirs at law of John Broadwater, a gunners mate in the Virginia Navy in the Rev. War. 27 Dec 1830. p. 216.

John D. Fields and William B. Fields are the only heirs at law of John Fields dec'd. formerly a steward in the Virginia Navy in the Rev. War. 27 Dec 1830. p. 216.

Thomas Chandler, a lieut. in the Virginia Navy at the time of his death, left Mitchel Chandler his eldest brother, Laban Chandler and Littleton Chandler younger brothers and Catherine Chandler his sister then his only heirs at law. The said Littleton Chandler is now living. Sarah P. Burton, wife of John B. Burton is the only heir at law of the said Catherine Chandler, now dec'd. Mitchell Chandler, Thomas Chandler, Rosey Fitzgerald, Patience Harvey, Amelia Snead, wife of John Snead, Elizabeth U. Chandler and Amey Chandler, are the heirs at law of said Mitchel Chandler. Bagwell Chandler and Mary Chandler are the heirs at law of Laban Chandler who was a son of said Laban Chandler, dec'd., and Elizabeth, John, Josiah, Tabitha and Euphamia Chandler are the only heirs at law of Elisha Chandler, a son of said Laban Chandler the elder. 27 Dec 1830. p. 216.

Martha Henderson, wife of John Henderson, Mary Jackson, wife of Stephen Jackson, Nancy Taylor, wife of William Taylor and Sally Taylor, wife of Preson Taylor are the heirs at law of Elijah Boston who was a soldier in the Continental Army in the Rev. War. 27 Dec 1830. p. 217.

William Revell, John B. Revell, James R. Revell, Sally B. Revell, Elizabeth R. Guy and Nathaniel F., Catherine and Margaret Revell are the only heirs at law of John Revell, dec'd., formerly a gunners mate in the Virginia Navy in the Rev. War, the said William, John B., James and Sally B. Revell and Elizabeth R. Guy being children of said John Revell, and the said Nathaniel F., Catherine and Margaret being the only children of George C. Revell another child of John Revell. 31 Jan 1831. p. 220.

Ann H. P. Hall, wife of Henry H. Hall, is the only heir at law of John Pitt, dec'd., who was a surgeon in the Virginia State Navy in the Rev. War. 31 Jan 1831. p. 220.

John W. Snead of Beaver Co., Pennsylvania, is the only heir at law of Robert Snead, dec'd., formerly a surgeon in the Virginia Navy in the Rev. War. 31 Jan 1831. p. 221.

Nancy Lee, wife of Andrew Lee, formerly Nancy Lumber, Martha Melson, formerly Martha Lumber, James Lumber, Thomas Lumber, William Lumber and Jane, Samuel, William and Thomas Lumber, infant children of Samuel Lumber dec'd. are the only heirs at law of Thomas Lumber dec'd. formerly an officer in the Virginia Navy in the Rev. War, the said Nancy Lee, Martha Melson, James, Thomas and William Lumber and

Samuel Lumber dec'd. being the only children of William Lumber, dec'd., who was the only brother and heir of said Thomas Lumber, dec'd. 31 Jan 1831. p. 221.

Bagwell Topping, Nancy Scott, wife of Severn Scott, Leah Chandler, wife of William Chandler, Sally Walker, wife of James Walker, Betsey Parker, wife of Revell Parker, Jacob M. Ross and Susanna Hornsby are the only heirs at law of John Hornsby, dec'd., formerly a seaman in the Virginia Navy in the Rev. War; the said Bagwell Topping being the only child of Nancy Topping dec'd. sister of said Jno. Hornsby, the said Nancy Scott being the only child of Betty Hornsby, a sister of said John Hornsby, the said Leah Chandler, Sally Walker, Betsy Parker and Susanna Hornsby being children of Major Hornsby dec'd., a brother of said John Hornsby, and the said Jacob M. Ross being the only child of Molly Ross dec'd., another child of said Major Hornsby. 31 Jan 1831. p. 225.

Elizabeth Trader, wife of Parker Trader of the City of Philadelphia, Pennsylvania, and Thomas Underhill of Accomack Co., Virginia, are the only heirs at law of William Underhill dec'd. formerly a captain in the Rev. War. 28 Feb 1831. p. 229.

Margaret, Eliza and John Walker are the only heirs at law of Jacob Phillips formerly a boatswain in the Virginia Navy in the Rev. War. 28 Feb 1831. p. 237.

Jacob Phillips and Eliza Copes are the only heirs at law of William Phillips dec'd. who was a seaman in the Virginia Navy in the Rev. War. 28 Feb 1831. p. 237.

Levin Parker, Peter Parker, John Parker, Mary Ann Chandler wife of Edmund Chandler and Henry Stakes and James Stakes are heirs at law of Richard Parker dec'd. formerly a captain in the Virginia Navy in the Rev. War. 28 Feb 1831. p. 239.

Harriet Savage, wife of George Savage of John, and Edmund W. Chambers, are the only heirs at law of Hancock Chandler who was a seaman in the Virginia Navy in the Rev. War. 28 Feb 1831. p. 239.

Zorobabel Budd, William Budd, John Budd, McKeel Budd, John Budd, Jr. and James Haley are the only heirs at law of Thomas Budd dec'd.

formerly a seaman in the Virginia Navy during the Rev. War. 1 March 1831. p. 241.

Thomas Lilliston, Anne Lilliston, Edmund Lilliston, Samuel Nock, Sally Bowen, wife of James Bowen and Polly Nock are the only heirs at law of Covington Broadwater dec'd. formerly a midshipman in the Virginia Navy during the Rev. War. 1 March 1831. p. 241.

Covington Bennett, Roland Bennett, Samuel Bennett, Littleton Bennett, Polly Bennett, now of the City of Philadelphia, are the only heirs at law of William Bennett dec'd. formerly an officer in the Virginia Navy during the Rev. War. 28 March 1831. p. 249.

Catherine Moore, Elizabeth Custis, wife of William H., Rachel Rodgers, wife of William W., Elijah Boggs and James Boggs, William C. Boggs, Nancy Northam, wife of Custis, Peggy Parker, wife of John, Peggy Mason, wife of William, Jane and Lucy Boggs and Henry Boggs are the only heirs at law of Abel Boggs dec'd. formerly in service in the Virginia Line on Continental Establishment in the Rev. War. 28 March 1831. p. 249.

Peggy Bonwell, wife of Mckeel, George Salisbury, William Salisbury, George C. Salisbury, Elizabeth Salisbury, Mary Salisbury, Cassey Salisbury, Robert Salisbury, the children of Joshua Salisbury of Maryland, and the children of Sally Topping, wife of Smith Topping, are the heirs at law of Moses Salisbury who was an Armorer in the Virginia Navy in the Rev. War. 28 March 1831. p. 250.

William Willett, Thomas Ayres, Littleton Ayres and Henry Ayres are the heirs at law of Francis Ayres and Henry Ayres, soldiers in the Virginia Line on Continental Establishment in the Rev. War. 28 March 1831. p. 250.

Ann. T. Greer and Matilda, Sally, Ann, Mary, Lavinia, Clara and James Millechops are the only heirs at law of John Pettigrew dec'd. formerly a lieut. in the Virginia Navy in the Rev. War, the said Ann T. Greer being a dau. of said John Pettigrew and the said Matilda, Sally, Ann, Mary, Lavinia, Clara and James Millechops being the only children of Lavinia Millechops dec'd., another dau. of said John Pettigrew. 30 March 1831. p. 257.

Nancy Bull, wife of George, is the only heir at law of Thomas Snead dec'd. formerly a soldier in the Virginia Line on Continental Establishment in the Rev. War. 30 March 1831. p. 263.

William Copes, George Copes, William C. Dix, Elizabeth Dix, Molly Dix, William Dix, William and Richard Singleton are the heirs at law of Solomon Copes dec'd. formerly a soldier in the Virginia Line on Continental Establishment in the Rev. War. The said William Copes and George Copes being children of Thomas Copes dec'd., one of the children of Solomon Copes dec'd.; the said William C. Dix, Elizabeth Dix, Molly Dix being children of Elizabeth Dix, dec'd., formerly Elizabeth Copes, a dau. of said Solomon Copes; the said William and Richard Singleton being children of Henney Singleton formerly Henney Dix, a dau. of said Elizabeth Dix; the said William Dix being son of Isaac Dix, who was a son of Elizabeth Dix. 30 March 1831. p. 263.

Thomas C. Ames, Matilda J. Ames, James Fisher, Catherine Ward, William A. Christian, Margaret Ames, wife of Richard, Matilda Guest, wife of Richard, Shadrack T. Ames and Tabitha A. Ames are the only heirs at law of George Christian dec'd. formerly an officer in the Virginia Navy in the Rev. War. The said Thomas C. Ames and Matilda J. Ames being the only children of Sally Ames dec'd. a sister of the whole blood to said George Christian; the said James Fisher being the only child of Elizabeth Christian dec'd. a sister of the half blood to the said George Christian dec'd.; the said Catherine Ward being the only child of Catey Ames dec'd. a sister of the half blood to said George Christian dec'd.; the said William A. Christian and Margaret Ames being the only children of William Christian dec'd. a brother of the half blood to said George Christian; the said Mahala Guest being the only child of John Milby dec'd. who was the only child of Rosey Christian dec'd. a sister of the half blood to said George Christian dec'd. and the said Mahala Guest, Shadrack T. Ames, Tabitha A. Ames being the only children of Nancy Ames dec'd. a sister of the half blood to said George Christian dec'd. 25 Apr 1831. p. 276.

John Pettigrew formerly of Accomack Co., Virginia, formerly a lieut. in the Virginia Navy in the Rev. War, left at his death Ann T. Greer and Leah Millichops his only heirs at law and Ann T. Greer is now living and Leah Millichops is dead, leaving as her heirs at law, Matilda, Ann P., Mary, Lavinia, Clara and James Millichops and Margaret Naudain and Sarah G. Cogwill. 2 June 1831. p. 294.

Patience Lumber dec'd., widow of William Lumber dec'd., who was formerly a gunner in the Virginia Navy in the Rev. War is now dead. The said William Lumber at his death the following children: Martha who is now widow of Noah W. Melson; Nancy now the wife of Andrew Lee, and Samuel, William, James and Thomas Lumber, all of whom are now living except the said Samuel Lumber, who has since died intestate leaving four children: Jane, William, Thomas and Samuel Lumber and not other children. 28 June 1831. p. 310.

Nanny Melson, widow of Levin Melson, who was formerly a carpenter in the Virginia Navy in the Rev. War, is now dead. James Milliner Melson who is commonly called James Melson, the son of said Levin Melson is now living; Amey the dau. of said Levin Melson died intestate leaving Nancy White her only child; Bridget, dau. of said Levin Melson died intestate leaving Levin Lewis her only child; Rachel Melson, dau. of said Levin Melson has since died intestate and without issue; Noah Wyatt Melson commonly called Noah Melson has since died intestate leaving four children: William Henry Melson called Henry Melson, Cassey sometimes called Kessey, Thomas sometimes called James Thomas, and Samuel Melson, all of whom are minors except the said Henry Melson. 28 June 1831. p. 310.

Thomas Underhill of this co. and Elizabeth Trader, wife of Parker Trader of Philadelphia, are the only heirs at law of William Underhill who was sometimes called William Undsill, who was formerly a captain in the Virginia Navy in the Rev. War; the said Elizabeth Trader being the only child of Sarah Underhill or Undsill and the said Sarah and Thomas being the only children of Micajah Underhill or Undsill who was the only brother of said William Underhill or Undsill, and who died before the said William Underhill. The said William Underhill or Undsill at his death left no parents or children or descendants of children and no brother or sister nor descendants of a brother or sister except the said Sarah and Thomas Underhill or Undsill; the said Thomas and Sarah Underhill or Undsill are the same persons who are residuary devisees in the will of said William Underhill; the said Sarah Underhill always resided and died in this co. intestate leaving the said Elizabeth now the wife of said Parker Trader her only child. 28 June 1831. p. 311.

The following died intestate, all in the Virginia Navy during the Rev. War:
Laban Bayly, formerly a quarter master.
Levin Bird, formerly a pilot.

John Cropper, formerly a carpenter.
Robert Webb, formerly a pilot.
John Broadwater, formerly a gunner.
Covington Broadwater, a midshipman.
John Fields, a steward.

Isaac Walters, formerly a boatswain in the Virginia Navy during the Rev. War died intestate. Patty Thomas and Sally Walters are the only heirs at law. 28 June 1831. p. 313.

Beverly Copes, formerly a midshipman in the Virginia Navy in the Rev. War died intestate. Parker Copes, Beverly Copes, Nancy Merrill, Bersheba Martin wife of --- Martin of Philadelphia and Hetty Copes are the only heirs at law of said Beverly Copes.

Ordered that the guardian of Anna, Washington, Mary, Richard T. and Annathy Ames, heirs of Levin Bird, sell and assign all the scrip to which the said heirs may be entitled for the military services of the said Levin Bird as a pilot in the Virginia Navy in the Rev. War.

Ordered that the guardian of the heirs of Isaac Walters sell and assign all the scrip to which the said heirs may be entitled for the military services of said Isaac Walters as boatswain in the Virginia Navy in the Rev. War.

Ordered that the guardian of Hetty Copes, one of the heirs of Beverly Copes, a midshipman in the Virginia Navy in the Rev. War, sell and assign all the scrip to which she may be entitled for the military services aforesaid of said Beverly Copes.

Ordered that the guardian of James Hickman and Mary Lilliston heir of John Cropper, carpenter in the Virginia Navy in the Rev. War, sell and assign all the scrip to which they may be entitled for the services of John Cropper.

Ordered that Thomas R. Joynes, guardian of Jane, William, Thomas and Samuel Lumber, sell, assign and transfer all the scrip to which they may be entitled as heirs of William Lumber, dec'd., for his services as gunner in the Virginia Navy in the Rev. War.

Ordered that James Melson, guardian of Levin Lewis, sell, assign and transfer all the scrip to which the said Levin may be entitled as one of the heirs of Levin Melson, dec'd., a carpenter in the Virginia Navy in the Rev. War. 28 June 1831. p. 314.

Ordered that Levin James, guardian to Thorowgood and Sarah Young, heirs of Robert Webb, formerly a pilot in the Virginia Navy in the Rev. War, sell, assign and transfer all the scrip to which they may be entitled for the services of the said Robert Webb as aforesaid. 30 June 1831. p. 322.

Alexander Lang who is said to have been a boatswain in the Virginia Navy in the Rev. War, was sometimes called Ling; his will was proved in this court by the name of Alexander Ling; he died 27 Apr 1820; Sally Lang who executed a power to Thomas M. Bayly and John Riley, a Justice of the Peace, is the widow and devisee of said Alexander Lang alias Alexander Ling. 30 June 1831. p. 325.

John Pitt, formerly a surgeon in the Virginia Navy in the Rev. War, left at his death no children, and no brother or sister except one brother, Robert Pitt and one sister Ann Pitt, and no descendant of any other brother or sister; the said Robert Pitt at his death left one child named Ann who has since died leaving only one child Ann H. Hall, wife of Henry H. Hall; the said Ann Pitt, sister of the said John Pitt afterwards married Robert Foreman and survived her said husband and died without issue in 1804, and her will was proved in this court 25 June 1804. Walter Bayne, named in the will of said Ann Foreman, has since died leaving six children: William D., George W., John F., Walter D., Colmore S. and Elizabeth, now the wife of Gideon Pierce, and the said William D. and George W. have since died childless and the said John F. Bayne has since died intestate leaving one child who died shortly after the death of the said John F. Bayne, and the said Walter D., Colmore S. Bayne and Elizabeth Pierce are now living. 25 July 1831. p. 332.

Robert White, Elizabeth Ross, wife of William Ross, and Margaret Hall, widow of Richard Hall, are the only children and heirs at law of Robert White dec'd. who was said to be formerly a midshipman in the Virginia Navy in the Rev. War. 25 July 1831. p. 338.

James Broadwater, formerly a quarter master in the Virginia Navy in the Rev. War died intestate. William Corbin, formerly a master at arms in the Virginia Navy in the Rev. War died intestate. 25 July 1831. pp. 334-5.

Lewis White, son of William S. White, dec'd., who was formerly a surgeon's mate in the Virginia Navy in the Rev. War, died before his said father and without issue. Gustavus White, son of William S. White, has since died leaving one child, Elizabeth Ann. 26 July 1831. p. 341.

Ann H. P. Hall, wife of Henry H. Hall, is the only child and heir at law of Matthew Bears (Beard) dec'd. who was the brother of John Bears dec'd. late of Centreville, Queen Anne's Co., Maryland. The said Ann H. P. Hall being the niece and one of the heirs of said John Bears. 29 Aug 1831. p. 353.

Moses Salisbury, formerly an armorer in Virginia Navy in the Rev. War, died intestate leaving no parents or children nor descendants of children. He left two brothers, John and Joshua, and one sister, Keziah. Said John Salisbury died intestate leaving five children: Sally who married Smith Topping of Elizabeth City Co., George, Peggy now the wife of McKeel Bonwell, Thomas who has since died intestate leaving four children: John, Coleburn, Caty wife of James Mister, and Nancy widow of Levin Savage and Robert who has since died intestate leaving six children: Mary, Eliza, George, Cassey, William and Robert. The said Joshua Salisbury died intestate leaving four children: Ezekiel who has since died intestate leaving James, Betsey and Elisha; the said Keziah died intestate leaving two children, Abram Somers, Jr. and Ezekiel Somers who is dead leaving one son Abram Somers, Jr. 30 Aug 1831. p. 361.

Elizabeth Phillips is the only child and heir at law of Solomon Powell dec'd. who was a seaman in the Virginia Navy in the Rev. War. 30 Aug 1831. p. 362.

James S. Corbin, Mary Jane Corbin and Sarah Ann Corbin are the only heirs at law of George Stewart who was muster master, paymaster and purchasing commissary to the Accomack and Diligence Galleys in the Virginia Navy in the Rev. War. 30 Aug 1831. p. 362.

Rebecca Joynes, widow of Edward Joynes, William Joynes son of Edward, and Edward Collins, son of Nancy Collins, formerly Nancy Joynes, dau. of said Edward Joynes, are the only heirs at law of Edward Joynes who was a seaman in the Virginia Navy in the Rev. War. 31 Aug 1831. p. 366.

John Pettigrew, a lieut. in the Virginia Navy in the Rev. War, was the only heir at law of Gavin Pettigrew, who was a seaman in the Virginia

Navy in the Rev. War, and said Gavin Pettigrew died intestate. 26 Sept 1831. p. 371.

Mary Stephens is the only heir at law of Stephen Stephens and Simon Stephens dec'd., both of whom were in the Virginia Navy.

Levin Beach, James Beach, Molly Beach and John Belote are the only heirs at law of John Beach, late a soldier in the 9th Va. Regt. 26 Sept 1831. p. 379.

David Ashby, who served in the Rev. War, died without issue; James Ashby who also served in the Rev. War has not been heard from for the last 15-20 years. They left brothers and sisters as follows: John Ashby, Molly Ashby and Tamar Ashby. John Ashby left five children who have issue: John Ashby, Sally Ashby, Samuel Ashby, Ezekiel Ashby and Elizabeth Ashby; John Ashby died leaving Smith Ashby and Sally Floyd, wife of Thomas, his only heirs at law; Sally Ashby married Jesse Ames and died leaving three children: John A. Ames, Thomas Ames and Jesse Ames; the said Jesse is dead and left three children: Emily Ames, Georgianna Ames and Virginia Margaret Ames; Samuel Ashby is dead and left four children: Juliet Robins, wife of Arthur, Elizabeth Mears, widow of William, Levi Ashby and Mary Asbhy; Ezekiel Ashby died leaving four children: Margaret Ashby, Elizabeth Ashby, Washburn Ashby and David Ashby; Elizabeth Mears is dead leaving three children: William D. Mears, Sally Mears and Elizabeth Mears. Molly Ashby married William Beach and both died leaving Ezekiel Beach their only child; the said Ezekiel Beach died leaving one child: Molly Beach who married Littleton Willis; the said Molly Willis is dead leaving Elizabeth Willis her only heir at law. Tamor Ashby married Robert Savage and died leaving children unknown. Said Smith Ashby, Sally Floyd, John A. Ames, Thomas Ames, Emily Ames, Georgianna Ames, Virginia M. Ames, Juliet Robins, Elizabeth Mears, Levi Ashby, Mary Ashby, Margaret Ashby, Ezekiel Ashby, Washburn Ashby, David Ashby, William D. Mears, Polly Mears, Elizabeth Mears, Elizabeth Willis and the children of Tamar and Robert Savage are the only heirs at law of David and James Ashby, both of whom were soldiers in the Army of the Rev. War. 27 Sept 1831. p. 381.

Caty Gibbons, wife of James Gibbons, is the only child and heir at law of Abel Wright, soldier in the Rev. War.

Nathaniel Vesick is the only son and only heir of Moses Vesick, soldier in the Rev. War.

Molly West, wife of Thomas West and Nancy Bishop, widow of Southey are the only heirs at law of Reuben Bonwell, soldier in the Rev. War.

Hetty, Polly, Nancy, Asa, Leah, William and Robert Lilliston are the only children and heirs at law of William Lilliston who was formerly a soldier in the Rev. War and to whom a pension was granted 9 July 1818, No. 6875.

Margaret Bunting, Sally Bunting, Thomas Bunting, Susan Bunting and Rachel Bunting, wife of Richard, are the only children and heirs at law of Solomon Bunting, dec'd.

Kendall Richardson is the only son and heir at law of William Richardson dec'd. 27 Sept 1831. p. 382.

Abel Bradford, soldier in the Rev. War, died without issue, leaving one brother named Zephania Bradford, who died leaving five children: Mary, Jane, Abel, Betsey and Esther. Mary Bradford married John Mears (K) and is dead leaving seven children: Abel Mears, Elizabeth Mears, Mary Downing, wife of John, John Mears (K), James Mears, William Mears and Robert Mears. Betsey Bradford married John Mears of Richd., died leaving three children: Elizabeth Barnes, widow of William, Charlotte Bell, wife of James and Frederick Mears. Esther Bradford married Littleton Lecato and died leaving four children: Nathaniel Lecato, William Lecato, Littleton Lecato and John Lecato. Jane Bradford married John Bundick and is living. Abel Bradford is living. The aforesaid issue of Zephaniah Bradford are the only heirs of said Abel Bradford. 27 Sept 1831. p. 382.

Jacob Chance, soldier in the Army of Rev. left no children or issue. He left two brothers named William Chance and Elijah Chance. Said William left children not known to the deponent. Elijah Chance left one son named Elijah died leaving six children: Nancy Harmon, wife of Abel K., William Chance, Elijah Chance, John Chance, Thomas Chance and Margaret Chance. The children of William Chance, wherever they may be, and the aforesaid children of Elijah Chance are the only heirs of said Jacob Chance. 27 Sept 1831. p. 382.

Thomas Bonwell or Bonnewell, formerly an officer in Virginia Navy went to sea about 40 years ago and has not been heard from since that time, and is supposed to have been drowned. He left no children or descendants; he left six brothers and sisters of the whole blood: Richard, Southey, Betsey, McKeel, Sarah and Peggy. Richard Bonnewell, brother of Thomas, died some years ago leaving one child his only heir: Rosa who married Savage Crippen, both of whom died leaving John Crippen and Narcissa Crippen, the only heirs at law of the said Rosa Crippen and of said Richard Bonnewell. Southy Bonnewell, brother of Thomas is dead leaving Levin Bonnewell and Anna Snead, wife of Isaac Snead his only children and heirs at law. Betsey Bonnewell, sister of Thomas, married James Bonnewell, both of whom died some years since leaving Robert, Sally, Betsey, Elijah and Clement Bonnewell their only children and heirs. Robert son of Betsey is dead leaving Betsey Bull, wife of John Bull, Jr., his only dau. and heir at law. Sally Bonwell, dau. of Betsey is living. Betsey Bonwell, dau. of Betsey, married McKeel Wise and is now his widow. Elijah Bonwell, son of Betsey is dead leaving Clement, Harriett, Tabitha, Sally and Leah Bonwell his only children and heirs at law. Clement Bonwell, son of James and Betsey, is dead, leaving Betsy East, widow of Richard, James Bonwell, Robert Bonwell and Elijah Bonwell his only children and heirs at law. McKeel Bonwell, brother of Thomas, died leaving the following children: McKeel, Peggy and Elizabeth; McKeel, son of McKeel, is living; Peggy married William West and died leaving Polly West her only heir at law; Elizabeth is living. Peggy Bonwell, sister of Thomas, married James Lewis and died leaving three children: Peggy, Sally and William; Peggy Lewis married Robert Russell and died leaving children unknown; Sally married Laban Gunter and is now his widow; William Lewis died some years since leaving two children: William and John, both of whom are dead leaving Sophia Garner, wife of William, their only heir at law. Sarah Bonwell, sister of Thomas, married first George Russell and last Smith Melson, all of whom are dead; Sarah left by George Russell two children: Robert and Peggy; Robert is living and Peggy married Benjamin West and died leaving children unknown; said Sarah left by Smith Melson one dau: Scarborough Turnall, widow of Thomas Turnall. 27 Sept 1831. p. 382.

The following persons who served in the Virginia Navy in Rev. War died intestate: Hancock Chambers, a seaman; Jacob Phillips, an officer; William Phillips, a seaman; Hancock Chambers, a seaman.

Ordered that Henry Walker, guardian of John P. Walker, sell, assign and transfer all the scrip to which the said John P. Walker may be entitled as one of the heirs of Jacob Phillips, who was an officer in the Virginia Navy in the Rev. War. 31 Oct 1831. p. 387.

William, Thomas, Betsey and Mary Topping are the only children and heirs of Sally Topping, one of the heirs at law of Moses Salisbury, an armorer in the Virginia Navy in the Rev. War. 31 Oct 1831. p. 391.

Levin Parker, Peter Parker, John Parker, Mary Ann Chandler, wife of Edmund Chandler, Henry Stakes and James Stakes are the only heirs at law of Richard Parker, dec'd., formerly a captain in the Virginia Navy in the Rev. War. 31 Oct 1831. p. 392.

Ordered that John D. Fields, guardian of William B. Fields, sell, assign and transfer all the scrip to which said William B. Fields may be entitled as one of the heirs of John Fields, an officer in the Virginia Navy in the Rev. War.

Ordered that Middleton Mason, guardian of James Salisbury, one of the heirs of Moses Salisbury, assign, sell and transfer all the scrip to which said James Salisbury may be entitled for the services of said Moses Salisbury as an officer in the Virginia Navy in the Rev. War. 28 Nov 1831. p. 400.

Ordered that Thomas M. Bayly, guardian of Cassey Salisbury, sell, assign and transfer all the scrip to which she may be entitled as one of the heirs of Moses Salisbury, an armorer in the Virginia Navy in the Rev. War. 26 Dec 1831. p. 419.

John Harris, dec'd., who was a commissioned officer in the Virginia Navy in the Rev. War. Admin. on his estate granted to Thomas M. Bayly. 26 Dec 1831. p. 419.

William Taylor, late a Rev. pensioner, died 27 Nov last; Rachel Taylor is his widow. 30 Jan 1832. p. 429.

Samuel Russell, late a Rev. pensioner, died 4 Feb 1831.

Solomon Parks, late a Rev. pensioner died 27 Dec last; Nancy Parks is his widow. 30 Jan 1832. p. 431.

Caty Scott is the child and only heir at law of William Doe, formerly a soldier in the Rev. War. 27 Feb 1832. p. 441.

Levin Walker on whose estate William Parramore, Jr. qualified as admr. de bonis non with the will annexed, on 27 Dec 1830, is the same Levin Walker who was a lieut. in the Virginia State Line in the Rev. War; said Levin Walker died 21 Oct 1798. 27 March 1832. p. 450.

Southy W. East, Severn East and Mary Bloxom, wife of Elijah Bloxom, are the only heirs at law of Southy East and Nehemiah Walker dec'd. who were in the Army of the Rev. from Virginia. 27 March 1832. p. 451.

Catharine (alias Kittura) Weston, wife of William Weston, now resident of Utica, New York, and lately residents of Hartford, Connecticut, and Stephen Drummond and Cary Drummond of Elizabeth City Co., Virginia, are the only heirs at law of Jesse Cannon who was a lieut. in the Virginia Navy in the Rev. War, and of Luke Cannon who was a midshipman in the Virginia Navy in the Rev. War; the said Catharine West being a child of Elizabeth Drummond dec'd., formerly Elizabeth Cannon, who was a sister of said Luke and Jesse Cannon, and the said Stephen and Cary Drummond being the only children of Stephen Drummond dec'd. another child of said Elizabeth Drummond; the said Luke Cannon and Jesse Cannon left at their deaths no parents or children nor descendants of children and no brother or descendants of a brother and no other sister nor descendants of a sister except the said Elizabeth Drummond, formerly Elizabeth Cannon. Said Elizabeth Drummond left no children or descendants of children except the said Catharine or Kittura Weston and Stephen Drummond. 30 March 1832. p. 462.

Edward C. Revell, one of the children and devisees of John Revell, dec'd., who was formerly a gunners mate in the Virginia Navy in the Rev. War, has died intestate and without issue, leaving as his next of kin and only heirs at law, his brothers and sisters, William Revell, John B. Revell, James Revell, Sally B. Revell and Elizabeth R. Guy, formerly Elizabeth R. Revell, and one nephew Nathaniel F. Revell and two nieces Catharine and Margaret Revell, the said Nathaniel F., Catharine and Margaret being the only children of George C. Revell dec'd. who was a brother of said Edward C. Revell. 30 Apr 1832. p. 465.

James W. Melvin, Ibby Taylor, wife of Revelle Taylor, Barbara Kelley, Oliver Knox, John Knox, Albert Knox and Elizabeth Knox, are the only heirs at law of John Marshall, dec'd., an officer in the Virginia Navy in the Rev. War. 28 May 1832. p. 475.

Elijah Bayly, Molly Bayly, John Bayly and Betsy Bayly are the only heirs at law of Robert Bayly, seaman in the Virginia Navy in the Rev. War.

Agnes Bloxom, Nancy Bloxom, William Bloxom, George Bloxom, David Bloxom and Elijah Bloxom are the only heirs at law of George Bloxom, dec'd., seaman in the Virginia Navy in the Rev. War.

Betsey Bloxom, Rosey Bloxom and Rachel Bloxom are the only heirs at law of Stephen Bloxom, dec'd., seaman in the Virginia Navy in the Rev. War.

Elkanah Andrews, Jacob Andrews, Southy Rew, Isaac Andrews, Caty Hinman and Joice Andrews are heirs at law of William Andrews, seaman in the Virginia Navy in the Rev. War.

Edward A. Joynes and Sally Ames, wife of Samuel W. Ames, are the only heirs at law of Southy Mears who served in the Virginia Navy in the Rev. War.

Edmund Bundick is the only heir at law of Levin Bundick who served in the Virginia Navy in the Rev. War.

William C. Taylor is the only heir at law of Severn Taylor who served in the Virginia Navy in the Rev. War. 29 May 1832. p. 484.

Levin Moore, John Moore, Rachel Moore, Caty Crockett, widow of Asa and Susy Scott, wife of George, are the only heirs at law of Stephen Moore who served in the Virginia Navy in the Rev. War.

Fanny Hammons is the only heir at law of Tyre Hammons and Stephen Hammons, who served in the Virginia Navy in the Rev. War.

Henry Taylor is the only heir at law of Daniel Taylor, a sailor in the Virginia Navy in the Rev. War.

Skinner Collins, Thomas Collins, Sophia Collins and Rachel Smullings are the only heirs at law of Stephen Collins and James Collins who were seamen in the Virginia Navy in the Rev. War.

Nancy Marshall and Michael Marshall are the only heirs at law of Benjamin Marshall who served in the Virginia Navy in the Rev. War.

William, George, Henry and John Romas are the only heirs at law of Adam Romas, seaman in the Virginia Navy in the Rev. War. 29 May 1832. p. 485.

Branson Dolby, formerly a seaman in the Virginia Navy in the Rev. War died intestate.

Caty Jones and William Jones are the only heirs at law of Phillip Jones, dec'd., the said Caty being of the whole blood and said William of the half blood. 31 May 1832. p. 506.

Daniel Kelly, Richard Kelly and Nancy Smith, wife of Ralph, are the only heirs at law of William Kelly who was a soldier in the Rev. War. 30 July 1832. p. 534.

Levin Walker, lieut. in the Virginia State Line in the Rev. War, was a citizen of the co. at the time of his death, on 21 Oct 1798. Levin Walker left no children nor descendants of children living at his death except John B. Walker named in his will, which was proved in the District Court at Accomack Court House on 22 Oct 1798. Said John B. Walker died July 1826 and his will was proved in this court 31 July 1826; he left no child or descendant of a child living at his death, nor was Ann T. Walker, wife of John B. Walker pregnant at his death; said Ann T. Walker is now living in this co. 31 July 1832. p. 536.

Robert Snead, who was a surgeon in the Virginia Navy in the Rev. War, was a citizen of this county at the time of his death; he died intestate and left one child named John W. Snead who is now a citizen of Beaver Co., Pennsylvania. Said Robert Snead left no other child or descendant of a child. 31 July 1832. p. 536.

Nimrod Perkins states he enlisted as a drummer on board the Diligence Galley in the Virginia Navy in the Rev. War in 1777 and continued on board until she was laid up in 1781, and that he was on board and in the service more than three years. When he entered, Johannas Watson was captain, Richard Parker was 1st lieut. and Jesse Cannon, 2nd lieut. He was born in Accomack Co.; was a resident of the co. when he enlisted and when he was discharged. He received a Virginia Military Land Warrant for 100 acres and scrip for the same for said service. 31 July 1832. p. 537.

Peter Parker, admr. of Richard Parker, dec'd., is now a resident of Mexico. Upon the application of Levin Parker, John Parker and Edward Chandler, heirs at law of said Richard Parker, it is ordered that the letter of admin. heretofore granted to said Peter Parker be rescinded. On the motion of Thomas M. Bayly, with the consent of the said Levin Parker, John Parker and Edward Chandler, letters of admin. de bonis non were granted to said Thomas M. Bayly on the estate of said Richard Parker, dec'd. 1 Aug 1832. p. 542.

William Welburn, age 70 years, states he served in the militia of Virginia from age 16 until he became free from service by reason of age. He served as a soldier in a militia company in the co. aforesaid commanded by Capt. Thomas Marshall; was stationed at a fort then in this county at Musqueto Point, where a guard was kept; the said company was usually divided and 1/2 of it was stationed at Col. Corbin's landing and the other half remained at the said fort. He states he was in no regular battle but had several skirmishes with the refugees who kept the people in a constant state of alarm by the depredations. He was under arms over two years. After the war he commanded a militia company in the county many years. He was born in Accomack Co. John Cropper, John Poulson, Smith Snead and Thomas Parker were among the officers of the regular Army (9th Va. Cont. Regt.) from the co. where he served. 1 Aug 1832. p. 542.

Edmund Read, age 76 years, states he served in the militia of Accomack Co. from the time he was 16 years of age until free from duty by reason of age. During the Rev. War he served in Capt. Augustine Lecatt's and afterwards Capt. Americus Scarborough's Company of militia; he was engaged principally on the sea coast and on Chesapeake Bay coast. He performed service principally at Pungoteague and Andua. He was in only two engagements, one at Pungoteague and one at Parramore's landing, skirmishes in which the British attempted to carry away some vessels and succeeded in carrying away a brig belonging to Caleb Teackle. He was in actual service and under arms more than two years during the war. He was born in Accomack Co.; has no record of his age, although he understands that his birth was recorded in the parish register which cannot now be found. He was once taken prisoner by the British on Parramore's Beach but was detained only a short time. After the war he had command of a company of militia in the county and held command for many years. 1 Aug 1832. p. 543.

William Elliott, age 78, states he served in the militia of Virginia of Accomack Co. from the time he was about 16 years of age till free from duty by reason of age; during the Rev. War he served in Capt. William Polk's company. He states he was engaged principally on the sea and Chesapeake Bay coast in preventing the enemy from landing for the purpose of obtaining supplies and plundering and burning the houses of the inhabitants of this country. He performed duty at Upshur's Point, at Col. Parramore's Landing and the Metomkin Inlet and elsewhere as required. He was in actual service under arms at least 3 years during the Rev. War. He was born in Accomack Co. in 1754. 1 Aug 1832. p. 545.

Bowdoin Snead, age 72, states he served in the militia of Accomack Co., from the time he was 16 years of age until free by reason of age; during the Rev. War he served in Capt. Thomas Cope's Company and afterwards in the same company under Capt. Elisha Fitzgerald or Garrett and after the war under Capt. Samuel Waples. He was engaged principally on the sea coast and on Chesapeake Bay coast in keeping guard and preventing the enemy from landing for the purpose of obtaining supplies, plundering the country and committing depredations of every kind. He performed duty at the Block house on Col. Cropper's land and at the barracks near a wind mill on George Parker's land. He was in actual service under arms at least two years during the Rev. War. He was born in Accomack Co. 1 Aug 1832. p. 546.

John Harmon (of Henry), age 68, states he served in the militia of Virginia in Accomack Co. from the time he was about 15 years of age until free from military duty by reason of age. During the Rev. War he served in Capt. William Polk's company and in Capt. Ro: Coleburn's Company. He states he was engaged principally on the sea and Chesapeake Bay coast. He rendered service at Upshur's Point, at Parramore's Landing and at Metomkin Inlet, and elsewhere. He was in actual service under arms during the Rev. War at least 3 years. He was born in Accomack Co. in 1764. 1 Aug 1832. p. 547.

Houston Kellam, age 76, states he served in the militia of Virginia in Accomack Co. from the time he was about 16 years of age until he became free from military duty be reason of age. During the Rev. War he served in Capt. Nathl. Bell's company, frequently called out to keep guard and in actual service a considerable portion of time. He states he was engaged principally on the sea and Chesapeake Bay coast in preventing the enemy from landing for the purpose of obtaining supplies and plundering and burning the houses of the citizens of this co. He performed duty at Metomkin Inlet and other places in the county. He served under arms at least two years. He was born in Accomack Co. ca. 1756. 1 Aug 1832. p. 549.

Matthew Floyd, age 69, states he served in the militia of Virginia from about the age of 16 until free from military duty by reason of age; during the Rev. War he served in Capt. Richd. Savage's Company of militia. He states he was engaged in defending points on the seaboard of this county and at one time he went to Hog Island and continued there 10 months without interruption in constant service and later was removed to the mainland and still continued service. He was in actual service at least one year. He was born in Northampton Co., Virginia, in 1763. 1 Aug 1832. p. 550.

Hilary Mears, age 73, states he served in the militia of Virginia in Accomack co. from the time he was 16 years of age until he was discharged by reason of age. During the Rev. War he served in Capt. William Polk's Company. He performed duty at Upshur's Point, Parramore's Landing, at Metomkin and other points. He served under arms at least 3 years during the Rev. War in Accomack Co. He was born in St. George's Parish in Accomack Co. 1 Aug 1832. p. 551.

Custis Bull, age 70, states he served in the militia in Virginia in Accomack Co. from the time he was 14 years of age until free from duty by reason of age. He was a drummer in the militia during the whole of the War. The militia were often called out. He acted as drummer for a year or two before he was liable to do military duty. He was principally engaged as a drummer when the militia kept guard at Col. Cropper's blockhouse and the barracks at George Parker's mill. He served in Thomas Cope's and Elisha Garrett or Fitzgerald's companies during the war. He served as a drummer 4-5 years; attended all alarms and during the time guard was kept. He was to attend constantly as there was no other drummer to relieve him; all the other drummers having gone into the Continental service. He believes he was the only drummer in the regiment of militia after the 9th Regt. went away. He was born and always lived in this county. 1 Aug 1832. p. 553.

Daniel Bull, age 73, states he served in the militia of Virginia from about the age of 16 years until free from duty by reason of age. During the Rev. War he served in Capt. Garrett's (sometimes called Fitzgerald's) company of militia. The militia was frequently called out. He was stationed for the most part at Barracks and Parker's mill, but was moved from point to point as occasion required to prevent the enemy from landing for the purpose of obtaining supplies and committing depredations. At one time the company was marched up to Salisbury, Maryland, by Col. Simpson to suppress the tories who were dispersed. He served at least 3 years. He was born in Accomack Co. in 1759. 1 Aug 1832. p. 554.

John Taylor, soldier in the Rev. War died intestate. 27 Aug 1832. p. 562.

The children of Robert Garrett of Boston, whose names are unknown to the Court, Susan Johnson, wife of Elijah C. Johnson of Somerset Co., Maryland, and Elizabeth Bloxom, wife of Leml. Bloxom of Accomack Co., are the only heirs at law of Elisha Fitzgerald, alias Garrett, a soldier in the Rev. War. 27 Aug 1832. p. 562.

Tyre Harmons, seaman in the Virginia Navy in the Rev. War was sometimes called Tyre Hammond; Fanny Hammons is his only heir at law.

Stephen Harmons, seaman in the Virginia Navy in the Rev. War was sometimes called Stephen Hammons; Fanny Hammons is his only heir at law. 27 Aug 1832. p. 563.

Thomas Robins, age 73, states he served in the militia of Virginia from about the age of 16 until he was released from service by reason of age. He mustered in a company commanded by Capt. Shadrack Ames. He states he was engaged principally in guarding the coast on the Chesapeake Bay between Occohannock and Naswadix in Northampton Co., but rendered service at other places. He served at least 3 years. He was born in Northampton Co., Virginia, 7 July 1759; lived in Northampton Co.; has resided in this county for the last 47 years, moved here from Northampton. Thomas Parker, Nath'l Darby, Levin Joynes and John Cropper were in the regular Army in Northampton at the time he rendered service as a member of Capt. Ames' company of militia. On one occasion he was under the command of said Thomas Parker who was in the 9th Regt. Regular Army for the purpose of retaking some American property that had been taken by the enemy, and after the object was achieved he was again under the command of Capt. Ames. 28 Aug 1832. p. 568.

John Phillips, age about 70, states he served upwards of 2 years, in a company commanded by Capt. William Polk and attached to a regiment commanded by Col. William Parramore. He remained in the service until the end of the Rev. War. He was stationed most of his time on Watchapreague near the sea coast, in Accomack Co. but frequently marched from place to place. He was born in 1762 in Accomack Co. 28 Aug 1832. p. 571.

Jacob Sparrow, age about 68, states he was enrolled in 1780; served in the militia of Accomack Co., from the time he was 16 years of age until he was free from duty by reason of his age. He served during the Rev. War under Capt. Jesse Dickerson and Lieut. Thomas Sandford of the militia. Generally about 15-20 of each company kept guard at a time. He kept guard on Pocomoke River at Chincoteague and at Col. Cropper's barracks; he believed he served two years. He was born in 1764; always lived where he now lives. He enrolled in 1780 and subject to be called out at a moment's warning. He was acquainted with Col. Cropper, Major Poulson, Capt. Gilchrist and Col. Levin Joynes. 28 Aug 1832. p. 574.

William Harrison, age 73, states he entered the service of the Virginia militia in 1776 and continued in service for about four years; he served in the company commanded by Capt. R. Coleburn, attached to Col. William Parramore's regiment. Maj. James Spyers belonged to the said regiment. He was stationed most of his time on Wachapreague and Metomkin creeks in Accomack Co. but frequently marched from place to place in the county. He was born in 1759 in Accomack Co. 28 Aug 1832. p. 575.

Berry Hickman, age 69, states he served in Thomas Cope's and William Parker's companies in the militia of Accomack during the Rev. War from the time he was age 16 until he was free from duty by reason of age. He lived as an apprentice at Sergeant Grinall's during most of the War and was often sent by him to aid in summoning the men to arms when alarms were given. He thinks he served more than two years. He kept guard at Col. Cropper's barracks or blockhouse and other places, but never marched out of the county. Refers to his oldest child. 28 Aug 1832. p. 576.

The court declares that Jonathan Phillips of Accomack Co. was a Rev. soldier. 28 Aug 1832. p. 578.

Benjamin Colonna, age 69 and about 6 months, states he entered the Virginia Militia in 1779; served for two years; he served in Capt. Americus Scarbrough's company, attached to the regiment of Col. William Parramore and Major Savage. He was stationed most of his time on Craddock and Occohannock Creeks in Accomack Co., but frequently marched from place to place in said county. He was born in 1763 in Accomack Co. Since the Rev. War he has resided ten years in Northampton Co., Virginia. 28 Aug 1832. p. 578.

Charles Boothe, Scarburgh Melson, wife of James and Tabitha Snead are the only heirs at law of Alexander Harrison, a soldier in the Rev. War. 28 Aug 1832. p. 580.

James Colony, son of George, and Samuel Hickman and Polly Hickman, children of Polly Hickman, formerly Polly Colony, dau. of George Colony, are the only heirs at law of George Colony, a soldier in the Rev. War. 28 Aug 1832. p. 580.

Susan Chandler, widow of Littleton Chandler, states he died 4 July last. She believes he served over two years in the Rev. War, entering the service in 1777. Her husband resided all his life in Accomack Co. He was born March 11, 1761. 28 Aug 1832. p. 581.

Richard Wimbrough, age 70, states he served under Capt. Richard Justice, whose company was attached to the 2nd Regt. Virginia, to the end of the War and kept guard at Assawoman Creek and other places; was called on guard at a place called the Block House; served, he believes, upwards of two years. He was born in Accomack Co. in 1762; refers to his apprenticeship. 28 Aug 1832. p. 582.

Maddox Fisher, age 73, states he enlisted in a company of militia commanded by Capt. Wm. Christian in Jan 1777 and remained in the company about two years, and then went up to Accomack Co. to live and was enrolled in a militia company commanded by Capt. Wm. Justice 1 Jan 1779 and continued in said company until the end of the War. He was born in Northampton Co., Virginia, June 1759. 28 Aug 1832. p. 583.

Robert Chase, age 71, states he enrolled in a militia company commanded by Capt. John Moore in May 1777, attached to the 2nd Regt. of Virginia Militia. He kept guard on both sea and bay side of the county on Folly Creek and a fort called the Block House on Pocomoke River, also Assawoman and other places and on Hog Island where they had an engagement with several barges of the enemy and took one of their boats; on many alarms and marches; served 2-3 years. He was born in Accomack Co. 1 Jan 1761. His parents and his sister always told him that he was ten years the oldest. 28 Aug 1832. p. 583.

Elkanah Andrews, age 67, states he enlisted on board the galley called the Accommack commanded by Capt. William Underhill in 1777, he thinks; he served as a sailor until same was dismantled and her crew discharged which he thinks was in the winter of 1780-81. The said galley cruised mostly in the Chesapeake Bay and on the sea side of this peninsula while in service. The galley was built principally for the defence of the counties of Accomack and Northampton and stationed mostly in the waters of those counties; was never in any battle. He has proved his services heretofore and been allowed the quantity of land due as bounty from the state of Virginia for three years service in the Virginia Navy as a seaman. He was discharged when the galley was laid up. He was born in Accomack Co. 29 Aug 1832. p. 588.

John Parkes, Sr., age 76, states he volunteered in a company commanded by Thomas Bayly and served in said company attached to the 2nd Regt. Virginia Militia; he served in said company except 18 months when he was a soldier in the Continental Line; he enlisted under Thomas Parker and was stationed at Pungoteague and at different places in Accomack Co. until the company marched to the North and then he was attached to said company commanded by William Riley which was a short time before his term of service was up with Parker. Then he kept guard on Folly Creek at a place called the Blockhouse and at Chessconnessex Creek and other places and marched with the company into Maryland as far as Salisbury where they subdued the tories and up the Bay in a boat as far as Hoopers Straits at another time and at Watts Island, Foxes Island. He thinks he was on duty in the said company in keeping guard and marches in quest of the enemy upwards of two years. He was born in Accomack Co. 4 Sept 1756. He volunteered first and afterwards enlisted in the Continental Line (9th Regt.); Thomas Bayly was first Captain, and Thomas Parker, William Riley and John Custis the next. He is known by Capt. Samuel

Waples, Robert Russell, John Drummond and William Lee. 29 Aug 1832. p. 589.

Thomas Lewis, age 73, states he enrolled in a company commanded by Thomas Bayly first, then by William Riley and last by John Custis to the end of the War, attached to the 2nd Regt. Virginia Militia. He entered service in Jan 1778 and kept guard both on sea and bay in said county at a place called the Block House on Folly Creek and at Henry's Fort and Chesconnessix Creek and Doe Creek and many alarms and marches at different times up the Bay as far as Hooper's Straits in boats and at Annemessic in Maryland to subdue the tories, but they fled after a few fires, and also on Watts and Foxes Island in pursuit of the enemy; served upwards of two years. He was born in Accomack Co. in 1759. 29 Aug 1832. p. 590.

ORDERS 1832 - 1836

James Davis, age 69, states he was born in Maryland 4 March 1762; his father moved to Accomack Co. when he was about 12 years old where he has lived here ever since. He was called into service in a company commanded by Capt. Thomas Marshall, attached to the 2nd Regt. Virginia Militia. He entered the service and went on guard in July 1777, the first time at Wallops Island where he was stationed most of the time. He also did duty at Musqueto Point on Pocomoke River and on Onancock Creek and other places. 24 Sept 1832. p. 5.

William Bennett, a soldier in the Continental Line in the Rev. War died intestate. Peggy Elliott, wife of Charles Elliott and Sinah Bennett alias Sinah Carmine, are the only heirs at law of said William Bennett. 25 Sept 1832. p. 16.

Thomas Bennett, a soldier in the Continental Line in the Rev. War, died intestate. Peggy Elliott, wife of Charles Elliott and Sinah Bennett alias Sinah Carmine, are the only heirs at law of the said Thos. Bennett. 25 Sept 1832. p. 16.

George Harman, a soldier in the Continental Line in the Rev. War. died intestate. Betsy, Comfort, Leah and Sarah Harman are the only heirs at law of the said George Harman. 25 Sept 1832. p. 16.

Samuel Owens, a soldier in the Continental Line in the Rev. War, died intestate. Jesse, Mary, Sally, Elizabeth, Milcah, Ann and Margaret

Wilkerson are the only heirs at law of said Samuel Owens. 25 Sept 1832. p. 16.

Jacob Rogers, a soldier in the Continental Line in the Rev. War, died intestate. Nancy Richardson is the only heir at law of the said Jacob Rogers. 25 Sept 1832. p. 16.

William Willis, a sailor in the Virginia Navy in the Rev. War, died intestate. William Willett, Sally Dix, wife of William Dix, Lovey Hogshire and Susan Hogshire are the only heirs at law of the said William Willis. 25 Sept 1832. p. 16.

Daniel Litchfield, an officer in the Virginia Navy in the Rev. War, died intestate. 25 Sept 1832. p. 17.

George Hall, a seaman in the Virginia Navy in the Rev. War, died intestate. John C. Hall and Mary Ann, Eliza and John Hall, infant children of George Hall the younger, dec'd., are the only heirs at law of said George Hall the elder; the said John C. Hall and George Hall the younger being children of George the elder. John C. Hall, guardian of Mary Ann, Eliza and John Hall, infant children of George Hall the younger, are ordered to sell, assign and transfer all the scrip to which there are entitled as heirs at law of George Hall the elder. 25 Sept 1832. p. 17.

John C. Hall, Mary Ann, Eliza and John Hall, Gilbert Hall and Sophia Copes, wife of Peter Parker Copes, are the only heirs at law of Ephriam Hall, who was a seaman in the Virginia Navy in the Rev. War. Said Ephriam Hall died intestate. 25 Sept 1832. p. 17.

George Bloxom, William Andrews and Joshua Perkins, seamen in the Virginia Navy in the Rev. War, all died intestate. 26 Sept 1832. p. 21.

Tully Clark, soldier in the Rev. Army died intestate. John C. Hall, Mary Ann Hall, Eliza Hall, John Hall, Solomon West and James West are his only heirs at law. 27 Sept 1832. p. 28

Sally Topping is the only child and heir at law of Major Topping a soldier in the Rev. War. Major Topping died intestate. 27 Nov 1832. p. 44.

Starling Collins is the only heir at law of Stephen Collins, seaman in the Virginia Navy in the Rev. War. Stephen Collins died intestate. 27 Nov 1832. p. 45.

Starling Collins is the only surviving son and devisee of James Collins who served in the Virginia Navy during the Rev. war. 27 Nov 1832. p. 45.

James Ashby, Rev. soldier, died intestate. 17 Nov 1832. p. 45.

Elisha Simpson, seaman in the Virginia Navy in the Rev. War died intestate. 27 Nov 1832. p. 45.

Henry Rodgers who served in the Virginia Navy in the Rev. War died intestate. Custis Hargis, Sally Hargis, John Hargis, Thomas Hargis, William Hargis, Margarett Hargis, Nancy Hargis, George Hargis and Sophia Hargis are the only heirs at law of said Henry Rodgers. 26 Feb 1833. p. 83.

James Taylor, Rev. Soldier, died intestate. Charles Taylor, Polly Taylor, John Mears Beach and Susanna Metcalf are the only heirs at law of said James Taylor. 26 Feb 1833. p. 83.

John Jester, who served in the Virginia Navy in the Rev. War, died intestate. James Jester, Elijah Jester, Rachel Turlington, Kendal Jester, Leah Jester, Anny Jester, Henry Wimbro and Griffin Wimbro are the only heirs at law of the said John Jester. 26 Feb 1833. p. 84.

William Joynes and Edward Collins are the only heirs of Edward Joynes and John Joynes, the said John Joynes having been a sergeant in the Army of the U.S. in the Rev. War and said Edward Joynes was a seaman in the Virginia Navy in the Rev. War. 26 March 1833. p. 99.

Jacob Edwards, age 72 and about 9 months, stated he entered the state militia in 1776; he served in a company commanded by Capt. Thomas Copes and afterwards in a company commanded by Capt. Elijah Garrett, attached to a regiment commanded by Col. Southy Simpson. He was stationed most of his time on Folly Creek, East Point on Onancock and on Wachapreague; he marched from Accomack Co. to Somerset Co., Maryland, to subdue the tories. He believes he was encamped and under arms for two years and six months as a private. He was born in 1760 in Accomack Co. 28 March 1833. p. 106.

James Walker, who was a seaman in the Virginia Navy in the Rev. War, died intestate. Nancy Melson is his sister and only heir at law. 28 March 1833. p. 109.

William Colony, Rev. soldier, died intestate. James Colony, Samuel Hickman and Polly Hickman are the only heirs at law of said William Colony. 18 March 1833. p. 109.

Elijah Boston, soldier in the Virginia Line on Continental Establishment in the Rev. War, died intestate. 29 Apr 1833. p. 111.

Sally P. Burton, wife of John B. Burton, is the only child of Caty Bagwell dec'd. formerly Caty Chandler who was a sister of Thomas Chandler dec'd. who was a lieut. in the Virginia Navy in the Rev. War. Caty Chandler at the time of her death was the wife of George P. Bagwell who is since dec'd. 27 May 1833. p. 122.

Rachel Bloxom, Betsy Marshall and Rosey Ling are the only heirs of Stephen Bloxom, seaman in the Virginia Navy in the Rev. War. 24 June 1833. p. 157.

James Davis, age 71, states he joined a militia company commanded by Capt. Thos. Marshall, attached to 2nd Regt Virginia Militia. He went on guard July 1777, the first time at Wallops Island for 4 weeks, the next term at Musqueto Point for 4 weeks and a term of 4 weeks at Pocomoke River. That year he was mostly stationed at Wallops Island and Musqueto Point and he kept 4 terms of two weeks each at other places and in each and every year from Jan 1778 to the end of the war, and one term at Pocomoke River and one at Wisherts Landing in each and every year from 1778 to the end of the war of 3 weeks each. He kept guard at many other places, sometimes one week, sometimes one day and was on many alarms and marches from Onancock Creek in the lower part of Accomack to the line of Maryland and once marched as far into Maryland as Salisbury to subdue the tories, but they ran after a few fires. He believes he did half as much duty and more in alarms and marches as he did at our regular places of keeping guard. He served 2 years and 9 months as a private. "We would have some sharp shooting with the barges and privateers when they would come in the creeks and inlets, and one time on Wallop's Island the enemy landed and spiked our cannon before we could get a sufficient force to drive them ..." He knew William Welbourn who belonged to Capt. Marshall's company during the Rev.

War. Davis' company mustered at Assawoman with the companies of Capt. Cropper, Capt. Snead and Capt. Gilchrist, attached to the 9th Regt. before they marched to the north in the continental service. He was born in Maryland on 4 March 1762; his father moved to Accomack Co. when he was about 12 years old where he has lived ever since. His age is recorded in a book which his brother Major had at the death of his father. His brother has now been dead for 10 years. He joined the militia under Capt. Marshall when he was about 15 years old with the consent of his father. 29 July 1833. p. 167.

Robert Russell, age 76, states he enlisted in the Army of the U.S. in 1776, in Capt. Thomas Snead's Company of Infantry (Arthur Teackle, lieut.; Wm. B. Bunting, ensign) and moved in the 9th Reg. from Virginia. He was born in Accomack Co.; was living in Accomack Parish when he enlisted and resided in Accomack Co. ever since he left the service. He marched from Accomack, through Maryland and Delaware, to Philadelphia, then from Philadelphia to join the army under General Washington; he was at Trenton, Princeton, --- Town and in the Jerseys; he was at the battles of Brandywine, Chestnut Hill, Iron Hill and at the Battle of Germantown where he was severely wounded in the groin and taken prisoner and put in the new jail in Philadelphia. From there he was put on a prison ship and taken to New York where he was kept until he was exchanged when he again went and joined the Brigade commanded by Gen. Mulenburg; he continued in service 4-5 years when he was honorably discharged. 28 Aug 1833. p. 191. Proved by the oath of William R. Custis, son of Thomas Custis, dec'd, who was an officer in the Virginia Continental Line in the Rev. War, and by Levin T. Joynes and Thomas R. Joynes, sons of Col. Levin Joynes, dec'd., who was an officer in the Virginia Continental Line in the Rev. War.

George Colony, Rev soldier, died intestate. James Colony, Samuel Hickman and Polly Hickman are the only heirs at law of the said George Colony. 28 Aug 1833. p. 193.

Adam Mason was on duty in the field and in garrison two years as a soldier in the militia of this county during the Rev. War, on duty as long or longer than Jacob Edwards, Custis Bull, Edmund Read, Daniel Bull, John Harrison and Bowdoin Snead, to each of whom a pension has been granted by the U.S. and in the same regiment in which said Adam Mason served. The same orders were issued with reference to: William Harrison; William Watson; Peter Rogers, dec'd. (application made by

Hester Rogers, widow of Peter Rogers, dec'd.); Jonathan Phillips. 25 Nov 1833. pp. 222-224.

Benjamin Beach who served in the Virginia Navy in the Rev. War, died intestate; Tabitha Beach Turlington is his only heir at law.

Selby Taylor, soldier in the Virginia Continental Line in the Rev. War, died intestate; Hessey Taylor is his only heir at law.

Knevit Taylor, soldier in the Virginia Continental Line in the Rev. War, died intestate; Hessey Taylor is his only heir at law. 28 Jan 1834. p. 245.

General John Cropper, late of this county, who was a lieut. col commandant in the Virginia Line on Continental Establishment in the Rev. War, left at his death the following children: Ann Cropper, now the wife of George W. Arbuckle; Eliza Cropper, now the wife of Joseph W. Gibb; Catherine B., now the wife of Augustus W. Bagwell; John W. Cropper; Thomas B. Cropper; and Covington H. Cropper - all of whom are now living. Said John Cropper also left one other dau. Margaret P. Bayly who has since died leaving six children: Thomas H., Ann D., Sally C., Elizabeth W., Margaret P. and William P. Bayly, all of whom are living. Sally, another child of the said John Cropper, married John Wise and died in the lifetime of her father, leaving four children: William Wise, Margaret D. P., now the wife of Tully R. Wise, Henry A. and John C. Wise, all of whom are now living except said William W. Wise who died intestate and childless in the lifetime of the said John Cropper. Catherine Cropper, widow of said John Cropper is now living. 28 Jan 1834. p. 247.

Sacker Bayly, who was a soldier in the Virginia Continental Line in the Rev. War, died intestate and Jacob M. Ross, Susan Ross and James Ross are his only heirs at law. 28 Jan 1834. p. 247.

The following men who served in the Virginia Navy in the Rev. War, died intestate: Jabez Taylor, Daniel Lewis, Elisha Madrid, William Miles, Levin Mariner, William Riggs, James Warrington, and John White.

The following soldiers who served in the Continental Line in the Rev. War, died intestate: John Bishop, Joseph Ewell, Bundick Hinman, Thomas Hastings, Galin Mariner, Miles Northam, George B. Riggs, George Riggs, Elijah Ross, John Wessells, Spencer Waters. 24 Feb 1834. pp. 249-50.

George Becket, sailor in the Virginia Navy in the Rev. War, died intestate leaving no children or descendants of children, and leaving as his next of kin and heirs at law, four sisters: Nancy, Betty, Rebecca and Mason Becket. Said Nancy Becket died intestate leaving five children: Solomon, Thomas, Peter, Mary and John Beavans, all of whom are now living. Said Betty Beckett died intestate leaving four children: Peter, Rachel, Rosey and Nanny Becket; said Rebecca Becket died intestate leaving three children: Rosey, Solomon and William Becket. The said Mason Becket is living. 24 Feb 1834. p. 251.

William Hays is the only heir at law of William Hays dec'd. who was a soldier in the Virginia Continental Line in the Rev. War. 24 Feb 1834. p. 253.

Elisha Conner, Peggy Taylor and Nancy Peacock are the only heirs at law of Ezekiel Conner dec'd, soldier in the Virginia Continental Line in the Rev. War. 24 Feb 1834. p. 256.

Levin Mariner, James Mariner, Susan Collins, Elizabeth Shay and Leah Tindal are the only heirs at law of Levin Mariner dec'd, seaman in the Virginia Navy in the Rev. War. 24 Feb 1834. p. 256.

Joseph Walker dec'd. who was a seaman in the Virginia Navy in the Rev. War, died intestate, leaving no children or descendants of children, and leaving as his next of kin and heirs at law three sisters: Elizabeth White, Mary Taylor and Susan Smith. Said Elizabeth White is dead leaving as her heirs at law: Robert White, Margaret Hall and the children of Betsy Ross who names are unknown. Said Mary Taylor is dead leaving as her heirs at law William C. Taylor. Said Susan Smith is dead leaving as her heir at law John Smith. 24 Feb 1834. p. 256.

Nancy Dod is the only heir at law of Lewis Linton, soldier in the Virginia Line in the Rev. War. 24 Feb 1834. p. 256.

Noah Belote, sergeant in the Virginia Line in the Rev. War, died intestate, leaving three children: James, Perry and Nancy. Said James Belote is now living; Perry Belote is dead leaving children whose names are unknown to the Court; Nancy married John Stephens and has since died intestate leaving children: James, William, Sally, Eliza, Rosey, Elizabeth and Sarey Stephens. 24 Feb 1834. p. 261.

The former order of this Court proving the heirs of Elisha Simpson is erroneous in that the name of Mary Munday should be Leah Munday.

Charles Belote, Sally Gardner, wife of William Gardner, Jr., Nancy Elliott, wife of George Elliott, and John Elliott [Belote?] are the only heirs at law of William Belote, soldier in the Rev. Army.

The same persons who were proved by a former order of this Court to be the heirs of Solomon Bunting are the only heirs at law of Lear or Leah Bunting, his widow and devisee. 1 April 1834. p. 274.

William Simpson, seaman in the Virginia Navy in the Rev. War, died intestate leaving one son Charles Simpson who died intestate leaving four children: Charles Simpson, Sinah Colony, Comfort Simpson and Betsy Simpson who are the only heirs at law of said William Simpson.

William Lee is the only son and heir at law of Andrew Lee, soldier in the Rev. War and said Andrew Lee died intestate.

Edward, Sally and Gilbert Minson, children of Sally Minson, wife of Samuel Minson, which said Sally was dau. of Charles Joynes, are the only heirs at law now living of Charles Joynes, soldier in the Rev. War.

Beadwell Ward and Kendal Groten are the only heirs at law of Edward Wise, soldier in the Virginia Line in the Rev. War.

Peter Delastatious and John Delastatious are the only heirs at law of Joseph Delastatious, soldier in the Virginia Line in the Rev. War.

William Walton, Sally Hayward, Peter Delastatious and John Delastatious are the only heirs at law of Peter Delastatious, soldier in the Virginia Line in the Rev. War.

William Walton, Sally Hayward, Peter Delastatious and John Delastatious are the only heirs at law of William Delastatious, soldier in the Virginia Line in the Rev. War.

Margaret, John and Eliza Budd are the only heirs at law of Major Budd, soldier in the Virginia Line in the Rev. War.

Elizabeth Trader is the only heir at law of George Clark, soldier in the Virginia Continental Line in the Rev. War.

Caty Taylor, wife of James is the only heir at law of Toby Bull, soldier in the Virginia Continental Line in the Rev. War. Daniel McAllister alias McOllister, is the only heir at law of Daniel McAllister alias McOllister, soldier in the Virginia Continental Line in the Rev. War.

Sally Nelson is the only heir at law of James Nelson, soldier in the Virginia Continental Line in the Rev. War.

Caty Beacham, John A. Gladding, Caroline Gladding and Sally Gladding are the only heirs at law of John Britman, soldier in the Virginia Continental Line in the Rev. War.

Leah Heath, John A. Nelson, Sally Nelson, wife of Edward, James Nelson, Margaret Nelson, Elizabeth Nelson and Susan Nelson are the only heirs at law of John Addison, soldier in the Virginia Continental Line in the Rev. War.

John, Sally, Betsy Warrington, Cassey Midcap, wife of Jesse Midcap, Mahala Wise, Henny Riley and Sally Lewis are the only heirs at law of John Elliot, soldier in the Virginia Continental Line in the Rev. War.

Tully W. Fisher, Henry W. Fisher, Susan Northam, Delight Christopher, John Northam, Henry Northam and Sally Hirmon are the only heirs at law of Thomas Fisher, soldier in the Virginia Continental Line in the Rev. War.

Sally Burton, wife of Garrison Burton, Catherine Bunting, wife of Solomon Bunting, Rachel Snead, wife of Charles S. Snead, William Elliott, Littleton Elliott and Thomas P. Copes are the only heirs at law of Teackle Elliott, soldier in the Virginia Continental Line in the Rev. War.

Nancy Kelly, wife of Daniel, Rachel Phillips, wife of John and George Cutler are the only heirs at law of John Rodgers or Rogers and of Robert Rodgers or Rogers, soldiers in the Virginia Continental Line in the Rev. War. 1 April 1834. pp. 275-76.

Margaret Spiers, William C. Bloxom, Sally Miles, wife of William, Polly White, wife of Thomas, Jacob Bunting, George Bunting, Matilda Spiers,

Polly Spiers, Maria Holcroft, Betsey Richardson, wife of James, James Shield, James Wharton, Elijah Chance, John Chance, Thomas Chance, Margaret Chance, Sally Delastatious, wife of Thomas C. Delastatious, Margaret Garrison, wife of Abel, Thomas Shield, Samuel Shield and Margaret Shield are the only heirs at law of Caleb Spiers, soldier in the Virginia Continental Line in the Rev. War. 1 April 1834. p. 277.

Milly Mears and Molly Tignor are the only heirs at law of Benjamin Taylor and Bartholomew Taylor, soldiers in the Virginia Continental Line in the Rev. War. 1 April 1834. p. 277.

James Stallings is the only heir at law of Dohicky Arundel, captain in the Virginia Continental Line in the Rev. War. 1 April 1834. p. 278.

William Harrison is the only heir at law of John Harrison, soldier in the Virginia Continental Line in the Rev. War. 1 April 1834. P. 278.

Rachel Tigner, Levin Beach, James Beach, Robert R. Lingo, Elizabeth Lingo and Maria Lingo are the only heirs at law of James Watkinson and William Watkinson, soldiers in the Virginia Continental Line in the Rev. War. 2 April 1834. p. 279.

Nancy Taylor and Rosa Justice, wife of Teackle Justice, are the only heirs at law of Giles Taylor, who served in the Rev. War. 2 April 1834. p. 279.

Edmund Beasly is the only son and heir at law of Smith Beasly, soldier in the Rev. War. 2 April 1834. p. 281.

John Robertson, Molly Tignall, George Mears, Edmund Mears, Thorowgood Mears, Maria Mears and the children of Lea Hamby, if any, and the children of Bartholomew Taylor the younger, if any, are the only heirs at law of Robinson Taylor, soldier in the Virginia Continental Line in the Rev. War. 29 April 1834. p. 289.

John Robertson, Molly Tignall, George Mears, Edmund Mears, Thorowgood Mears, Maria Mears and the children of Lea Hamby, if any, and the children of Bartholomew Taylor the younger, if any, are the only heirs at law of Bartholomew Taylor, soldier in the Virginia Continental Line in the Rev. War. 29 April 1834. p. 289.

Elizabeth Lewis is the widow of George Lewis, dec'd, soldier of the U.S. in the Rev. War to whom a pension was granted by the U.S. He died 9th of this month. 26 May 1834. p. 295.

John Ashby dec'd. left at his death the following children: John, Sally, Samuel, Ezekiel, David and Elizabeth Ashby. Said John Asby the younger died leaving three children: William Ashby, Smith Ashby and Sally Floyd, wife of Thomas Floyd; said William Ashby is dead without issue and said Smith Ashby and Sally Floyd are living. Sally Ashby, dau. of John, married Jesse Ames and has since died leaving three children: John A. Ames, Thomas H. Ames and Jesse Ames the younger; the said Thomas H. Ames is dead leaving Norvilla Ames, Edward Thomas Ames and John A. Ames his only children; said Jesse Ames the younger is dead leaving Emily A. Ames, Virginia M. Ames and Georgianna C. Ames his only children. Samuel Ashby, son of John, is dead leaving three children: Julia, wife of Arthur Robins, Elizabeth, widow of William Mears, Levi Ashby and other children whose names are unknown. Ezekiel Ashby is dead without issue. Elizabeth Ashby, dau. of John, is dead leaving children whose names are unknown. 26 May 1834. p. 297.

Elizabeth Lewis, one of the children and devisees of John Elliott, soldier in the Virginia Continental Line in the Rev. War, died intestate leaving four children: Cassey, wife of Jesse Midcap, Mahala, wife of John Wise, Henry Riley and Sally Lewis. Sally Elliott another devisee of said John Elliott died intestate leaving three children: John B. and Sally Warrington and Betsey Bonwell, wife of Heely Bonwell. Levin Elliott another devisee of said John Elliott died intestate and childless leaving the aforesaid children of Elizabeth Lewis and Sally Warrington as his heirs at law. 27 May 1834. p. 301.

Sally Gardener, wife of William, Nancy Elliott, wife of George and John Edwards are the children of Jacob Edwards as mentioned in the will of William Belote, soldier in the Virginia Continental Line in the Rev. War. Charles Belote, another devisee of said William Belote is now living; George Belote another devisee of said William Belote died intestate and without issue; the said Charles Belote and the children of said Jacob Edwards his only heirs at law. 27 May 1834. p. 302.

Polly Delastatious, widow of Peter, is dead. William Delastatious, son of Joseph, died intestate leaving Peter and John Delastatious his only heirs, and Polly, Esther and Betsey Waltham, devisees of Peter Delastatious died intestate leaving William Waltham and Sally Waltham, now Sally or Sarah Hayward, their only heirs. 27 May 1834. p. 302.

William Delastatious, devisee of Joseph Delastatious, died intestate and without issue and Ezekiel Delastatious has been absent from this county and unheard of for more than seven years and is supposed to have died intestate. William and Ezekiel left Peter and John Delastatious their only heirs at law. 27 May 1834. p. 302.

John Harris, formerly a captain in the Virginia Navy in the Rev. War, died in 1785. 27 May 1834. p. 303.

Molly Beach, Levi Beach, James Beach, Rachel Tigner, Robert R. Lingo and Eliza Lingo are the only heirs at law of James and William Watkinson who were soldiers in the Virginia Continental Line in the Rev. War. 28 May 1834. p. 304.

Rosa Schoolfield, wife of Wm., Lorenzo D. Parker, John F. Parker and Clement Parker are the only heirs at law of Thomas Parker (of Clement) alias Thomas Parker, Jr., a midshipman in the Virginia Navy in the Rev. War. 28 May 1834. p. 305.

Thomas Howard alias Hayward, midshipman in the Virginia Navy in the Rev. War, died intestate; Ezekiel, Mary, Nancy and Margaret Howard alias Hayward and Polly Trader, wife of Whittington Trader, are the only heirs at law of said Thomas Howard alias Hayward. 28 May 1834. p. 306.

Jacob Payne, Polly Phillips, Elener Payne, Betsy Bonwell, Handy Phillips, James Phillips, Polly Phillips, wife of Handy, are the only heirs at law of Jacob Phillips, seaman in the Virginia Navy in the Rev. War. 29 May 1834. p. 313.

Sally Perkins is the only heir at law of Joshua Perkins, seaman in the Virginia Navy in the Rev. War. 29 May 1834. p. 313.

Bundick Taylor, Jesse Taylor, Scarburgh Whealton, William Thorrington, John Mathews, Elizabeth Taylor and William Taylor are the only heirs at law of Jabez Taylor, an officer in the Virginia Navy in the Rev. War. 29 May 1834. p. 313.

John White, an officer in the Virginia Navy in the Rev. War, died without issue; he had one brother and two sisters: Robert White the brother of said John White left three children: Robert White, Margaret Hall and Elizabeth Ross; said Elizabeth Ross is dead and left several children whose names are unknown to the Court. Wealthy Jones, one of the sisters of the said John White, left the following heirs: Rebecca Marshall, wife of John T. Marshall, who is the only dau. of said Wealthy now living; Rebecca Marshall, wife of John S. Marshall, Sr., Sally Collins and Elizabeth Massey dec'd. were grand children of the said Wealthy Jones. Margaret Marshall, another sister of the said John White dec'd. left the following children and heirs: Solomon Marshall, William S. Marshall, Fanny Evans, Eulphamy Johnson and Charlotte Johnson; and said Margaret Marshall left the following grandchildren: Narcissa Delastatious and William Wilkerson and Solomon Wilkerson. The above are the only heirs of said John White. 29 May 1834. p. 313.

Elizabeth Marshall, wife of William, Rachel Bloxom, Rosey Land, wife of Alexander, are the only heirs at law of Stephen Bloxom, seaman in the Virginia Navy in the Rev. War. Stephen Bloxom died intestate. 29 May 1834. p. 314.

Elijah Bayly, son of Robert Bayly, who was a seaman in the Virginia Navy in the Rev. War, is dead. 29 May 1834. p. 314.

Jenipher Marshall, master in the Virginia Navy in the Rev. War, on board the Galley Accomack, died intestate in this county on 1 April 1792. Euphemia Walston, widow of Samuel Walston, dec'd., formerly Euphemia Marshall, is the only child and heir at law of said Jenipher Marshall, and she is the same person to whom, with her late husband, the State of Virginia in 1830 or 1831, granted bounty land for the services of said Jenipher Marshall as aforesaid. 29 July 1834. p. 336.

Betsy Northam, wife of William Northam (of E.), is one of the heirs at law of Thomas Fisher, soldier in the Virginia Continental Line in the Rev. War. 27 Aug 1834. p. 351.

Samuel Waples, late a pensioner of the U.S. for services as an officer in the Rev. Army, died 11th of present month; Sabra P. Waples is his widow. 29 Aug 1834. p. 353.

Edmund Bell and Nancy Johnson are the only heirs at law of James Bell dec'd. formerly a seaman in the U.S. Navy who died in New York about two years ago; the admin. on his estate has been granted this date to Nancy Johnson with consent of said Edmund Bell. 29 Sept 1834. p. 359.

Covington Bennett, one of the children and heirs at law of William Bennett, formerly a master in the Virginia Navy, is a citizen of this county. Littleton Bennett, another son and heir of William Bennett removed to Elizabeth City Co. and died within a few months past, having been married about 8-9 years and is supposed to have left infant children and heirs. Polly Bennett, Rowland Bennett, Samuel Bennett, the remaining heirs of William Bennett, are not now citizens of the Commonwealth. Said William Bennett died Dec 1802. 24 Nov 1834. p. 385.

Leah Rew and Elizabeth Riggs are the only heirs at law of William Riggs, seaman in the Virginia Navy in the Rev. War.

Mary Mason and Sally Young are the only heirs at law of Bundick Hinman, soldier in the Virginia Continental Line in the Rev. War.

Rachel, Elizabeth, Thomas and James Walters are the only children and heirs at law of Spencer Walters, seaman in the Virginia Navy in the Rev. War.

Jonathan, William, Elizabeth and Betsey Young are the only heirs at law of Joseph Webb, seaman in the Virginia Navy in the Rev. War.

Betsey, Isaiah and William Tunnell are the only heirs at law of Joseph and James Tunnell who were seaman in the Virginia Navy in the Rev. War. 24 Nov 1834. p. 385.

Betsey Belote is the only heir at law of John Collins, drummer in the Virginia Continental Line in the Rev. War. 26 Jan 1835. p. 396.

William C. Slocomb, Walter S. Slocomb, Thomas Slocomb and Charlotte Slocomb of this co. are brothers and sister of the half blood of Samuel B. Slocomb dec'd., late of the city of New Orleans, Louisiana, and formerly a citizen of this co. of which he was a native. 23 Feb 1835. p. 407.

Ralph Hinman, soldier in the Rev. War, died leaving Elizabeth, Fanny and Argyle Bloxom who were half brothers and sisters to the said Ralph Hinman and only heirs at law of said Ralph Hinman, and Elizabeth married Edward Bowdoin leaving Nancy Bowdoin, wife of David Mears, and she also left a son named James Bloxom who left two children: George and Elizabeth Bloxom, only heirs of James Bloxom, dec'd., and Fanny married Jacob White and is now dead leaving one child Lucretia who is now living and only heir of Fanny, and Argyle Bloxom is dead leaving Richard, Fanny and Sarah Bloxom who are still living and only heirs of Argyle Bloxom. 23 Feb 1835. p. 493.

Severn Scott, late a Rev pensioner, died 16 Nov last; Nancy Scott is his widow. 23 Feb 1835. p. 412.

Levin Wise, late a soldier in the Army of the U.S. (and on whose estate admin. has this day been granted to John G. Joynes) was formerly a resident and was a native of this co., and that admin. of his estate was granted to said John G. Joynes with the consent and approbation of the heirs of said Levin Wise. 29 April 1835. p. 437.

Edward and Gillett Minson are the only heirs at law of Sally Minson who died intestate, and who was one of the heirs of of Charles Joynes, sergeant in the Virginia Continental Line in the Rev. War. 27 July 1835. p. 493.

Tabitha Maddux is the only heir at law of John Johnson, seaman in the Virginia Navy in the Rev. War.

Nancy Miles is the only heir at law of William Miles, seaman in the Virginia Navy in the Rev. War.

Hetty Trader, Robert Bayly, Henny Bayly, Nancy Bayly, Polly Bayly and Betsy Bayly are the only heirs at law of Robert Bayly, seaman in the Virginia Navy in the Rev. War.

Arthur Selby and Candis Selby are the only heirs at law of Jack Selby, seaman in the Virginia Navy in the Rev. War.

Zadock Bayly, Robert Bayly, Henny Bayly, Nancy Bayly, Polly Davis, Polly Bayly and Anna Downing are the only heirs at law of Southy Bayly, seaman in the Virginia Navy in the Rev. War.

Stephen Hill is the only heir at law of Samuel Ramsey who served in the Rev. War.

John Russell, Thomas Russell, Robert Russell and Ann Read (wife of William P. Read) are the only heirs at law of William Russel who served in the Rev.War. 29 July 1835. p. 502.

Patty Massey (wife of John Massey), Thomas Waters and Sarah Waters are the only heirs at law of Isaac Waters who was a soldier in the Virginia Continental Line in the Rev. War.

Isaiah Tunnell, Elizabeth Corbin and Maria Marshall are the only heirs at law of William Tunnell and Joseph Tunnell who were seamen in the Virginia Navy in the Rev. War.

Elizabeth Mears, Sally Copes and James Barnes are the only heirs at law of Charles Copes who served in the Rev. War.

William Bloxom, David Bloxom, Elijah Bloxom, George Bloxom, Nancy Tatham (wife of Stephen Tatham) and Rachel Kelley (wife of James Kelley) are the only heirs at law of George Bloxom who served in the Rev. War.

John Wessells, Senr., William Wessells, Ephraim Wessells, James Wessells, Catherine Russell, Nancy Wessells, Ephraim Wessells (of N.), Elizabeth Ewell, Sarah Johnson, Catherine Wessells (of N.), Laura Wessells, Isaac Wessells, Nancy Hickman, George Russell (of George), Thomas Russell, James Russell, Lucretia Russell, Esther Russell, Elijah Russell, William Russell, Thomas Moore, Polly Moore, Isaac Starling, Anna Young, Ephraim Wessells, Senr., Sarah Ann Russell, Nancy Wessells, Catherine Young, Betsey Summers, Arthur F. Wessells, John Wessells, Jr., Richard Wessells, Ephraim Wessells, (of B.), Kessey Annis, Susan Annis, Margaret Young, Nancy Dix, Susan Wessells, Samuel Wessells, Delight Russell, Noah Russell, Mary Russell, Southy Russell, Ann Maria Onions, Susan Onions, Westly Onions, Levena Jane Onions and Raymond Melvin Parkes are the only heirs at law of John Wessells who was a soldier in the Virginia Continental Line in the Rev. War.

Rosey Lang (wife of Alexander Lang), formerly Rosey Bloxom; and Betsy Marshall (widow of William), formerly Betsy Bloxom, are heirs of Stephen Bloxom, who served in the Rev. War.

Benjamin Belote, John Belote, George Belote, Nancy Darby and John Lawrence are the only heirs at law of Robinson Mahorn, soldier in the Virginia Continental Line in the Rev. War.

Nancy Kelley, Rachel Phillips, George Cutler, Betsy Phillips, Anderson P. Bloxom, Rachel Garrison and Nancy Kellam are the only heirs at law of Anderson Parker, who was a soldier in the Virginia Continental Line in the Rev. War.

Nancy Ewell, Betsey Waters, Polly Gladding, John Taylor, Revell Taylor and Betsey Taylor are the only heirs at law of Airs Taylor, seaman in the Virginia Navy in the Rev. War.

Galen Hinman, Littleton A. Hinman, Colmore C. Hinman, Lewis Hinman, Alfred C. Hinman, John Bird and Ralph Hinman are the only heirs at law of Ralph Hinman and Baily Hinman who were soldiers in the Virginia Continental Line in the Rev. War. 29 July 1835. p. 503.

Ezekiel and Nancy Wimbro are the only heirs at law of John Wimbro the residuary devisee of Ebern Wimbro, seaman in the Virginia Navy in the Rev. War.

Timothy Colony and Southy Colony, soldiers of the Virginia Continental Line in the Rev. War, died intestate and Nancy, Sarah and Elijah Colony were their brother and sisters and only heirs law. Nancy is now Nancy Melson. Sarah married John Parkes and died intestate leaving Edmund Parks, Peter Parkes, Polly Stephens, John Willett, Betsy Parkes, Anna Landin, James Parkes, Sally Churn, Edmund Turnall, Robert Turnall and Sarah Turnall her only heirs. Elijah Colony (brother of Southy and Timothy) died intestate leaving Caty Colony, John Colony, Susan Colony, Comfort Thomas, Henry Colony, Sally Colony, William Colony, Elijah Colony, Thomas Bull, Elisha Bull, Fanny Bull, James Colony and John W. Colony his only heirs.

George Satchell and William Satchell, soldiers of the Virginia Continental Line died intestate and without issue leaving Southy Satchell their brother and only heir at law. George and Esther Satchell, children and devisees of Southy Satchell are both dead (the said Esther intestate), and Southy Satchell, grandson and devisee of Southy Satchell who was brother of George and William is living; George (son of Southy) left six children his only heirs: William, George, Sukey, Sippa, Polly and Sally, the last two of whom (Polly and Sally) have died intestate and without issue, leaving their brothers and sisters William, George, Sukey and Sippa their only heirs. George Satchell, son of George (who was son of Southy) died intestate leaving George and Jane Satchell his children and only heirs. Sippa (dau. of George son of Southy) died intestate leaving Mary Satchell and James Satchell her children and only heirs. William Satchell, George Satchell and Sukey Satchell (children of George son of Southy) are living; Esther Satchell dau. and devisee of Southy Satchell (brother of the soldiers) died intestate leaving Polly Stephens, Hetty Stephens (both living) and Betsy Colony her only heirs. Betsy Colony, dau. of Esther Satchell (who was devisee of Southy) died intestate leaving Zippa Colony, Polly Lewis, Esther Colony, William Colony, Betsy Colony, James Colony and Sukey Colony her only heirs at law.

Jesse Taylor, Evans Taylor, Henry Taylor, William Thornton and William Hays, together with other heirs whose names are unknown to the Court are the only heirs at law of Jabez Taylor who served in the Rev. War.

Daniel Shay and Rachel Walker (wife of John Walker) are the only heirs at law of Miles Northam who served in the Rev. War. 29 July 1835. p. 504.

John Gladding is the only heir at law of John Jenkins who was a soldier in the Virginia Continental Line in the Rev. War.

Elizabeth Hart and Parker Shreaves are the only heirs at law of Isaac Fisher, seaman in the Virginia Navy in the Rev. War.

Betsey Justice and Nancy Taylor are the only heirs at law of Giles Taylor, seaman in the Virginia Navy in the Rev. War.

Christopher Ball, John Ball, Samuel Ball, Levi Ball, William Ball and Elizabeth Richardson are the only heirs at law of James Ball and Seger Ball who were soldiers in the Virginia Continental Line in the Rev. War.

Levi Ball is the only heir at law of Merrill Paradise, soldier in the Virginia Continental Line in the Rev. War. 29 July 1835. p. 505.

Leah Collins of Kent Co., Delaware, is the only heir at law of Richard Pettigrew dec'd., seaman in the Virginia Navy in the Rev. War. Said Richard Pettigrew died intestate 5 Oct 1835. 28 Dec 1835. p. 563.

Ordered that the guardian of the infant heirs of Sacker Bayly, dec'd., sell, assign and transfer all the military land scrip to which they may be entitled for the service of said Sacker Bayly in the Rev. War.

Ordered that the guardians of the infant heirs of John Jester, dec'd., sell, assign and transfer all the military land scrip to which they may be entitled for the services of said John Jester in the Rev. War.

Ordered that the guardian of the infant heirs of John Hall, dec'd., sell, assign and transfer all the military land scrip to which they may be entitled for the services of said John Hall in the Rev. War.

Ordered that the guardian of the infant heirs of Ephraim Hall, dec'd., sell, assign and transfer all the military land scrip to which they may be entitled for the service of the said Ephraim Hall in the Rev. War.

Ordered that the guardian of the infant heirs of John Britnom, dec'd., sell, assign and transfer all the military land scrip to which they may be entitled for the service of said John Britnom in the Rev. War. 28 Dec 1835. pp. 563-64.

Agnes Drummond is the only heir at law of Betsey Stephens, sister of Simon Stephens, seaman in the Virginia Navy in the Rev. War.

Ordered that the guardian of Sally, Rosey, Elizabeth and Lovey Stephens sell, assign and transfer all the scrip to which they may be entitled as heirs of Noah Belote, dec'd, a sergeant in the 9th Va. Regt. on Continental Establishment in the Rev. War.

The Court approves that the guardian of Elizabeth Bonwell sell, assign and transfer all the scrip to which she may be entitled as one of the heirs of Thomas Bonwell, dec'd., sailing master in the Virginia Navy in the Rev. War. 29 Feb 1836. p. 578.

Susa Northam, one of the heirs of Thomas Fisher, soldier in the Rev. War, has died intestate leaving George Northam her only child and heir at law. Sally Hinman, another heir of said Thomas Fisher, has died intestate, leaving John Northam and Milcah Northam, wife of Henry B. Northam, her only heirs at law. 29 March 1836. p. 594.

ORDERS 1832 - 1836

James, John, William and Nancy Wessells are the only heirs at law of John Wessells, soldier in the Rev. War. 2 June 1836. p. 27.

Ordered that the guardian of the infant heirs of Tully Clark, soldier in the Rev. War sell, assign and transfer all the scrip to which they may be entitled for the services of the said Tully Clark.
Also same orders with reference to Timothy Colony's heirs; Southy Colony's heirs; George Satchell's heirs; Southy Satchell's heirs; Ralph Hinman's heirs; Baily Hinman's heirs; Caleb Spiers' heirs; James Ashby's heirs; Ayres Taylor's (a seaman) heirs.
25 July 1836. pp. 41-42.0

Lewis Hinman, one of the heirs of Ralph Hinman and Baily Hinman, soldiers in the Rev. War, died intestate; Littleton A. Hinman, Colmore C. Hinman and Alfred C. Hinman are the only heirs at law. 25 July 1836. p. 44.

James West, one of the heirs of Tully Clark, soldier in the Rev. War, died intestate and Solomon West is the only heir at law. 25 July 1836. p. 45.

Fanny Bull, one of the heirs of Timothy and Southy Colonna died intestate leaving Thomas Bull and Elisha Bull her only heirs. 30 Aug 1836. p. 53.

Samuel S. Stone is the only heir at law of David Gould, surgeon in the Virginia Continental Line in the Rev. War. 31 Aug 1836. p. 60.

George, Edward, Thorowgood and Maria Mears are the only heirs at law of Milly Mears, one of the heirs of Benjamin Taylor, soldier in the Rev. War. 31 Aug 1836. p. 60.

Ordered that the guardian of the infant children of Polly Colony, heir of Timothy and Southy Colony, who were soldiers in the Rev. War, sell, assign and transfer all the scrip to which they may be entitled as heirs of the said Timothy and Southy, soldiers as aforesaid.

The income of the estate of William, Susan, John and Elijah Colony, orphans of Polly Colony, dec'd., is $5.25. Ordered that Thomas H. Bayly, their guardian, spend the same on them.

Leah Rew and Betsey Riggs are the only heirs at law of George B. Riggs and William Riggs, seaman in the Virginia Navy in the Rev. War.

William Tunnell, soldier in the 9th Va. Regt. in the Rev. War, died intestate; Isaiah Tunnell, Elizabeth Corbin and Mariah Marshall are the only heirs at law of said William Tunnell.

Tabitha Maddox is the only heir of Joshua Johnson, a boatswain in the Virginia Navy in the Rev. War.

Nancy Taylor and Betsey Justice are the only heirs at law of Giles Taylor, seaman in the Virginia Navy in the Rev. War.

Molly, Nancy, John, Ephraim, James, William and Caty Russell are the only heirs at law of John Russell, soldier in the 9th Va. Regt. in the Rev. War.

Nancy Mariner is the only heir at law of Paban Mariner, seaman in the Virginia Navy in the Rev. War.

Nancy and Caty Miles are the only heirs at law of Thomas Taylor, seaman in the Virginia Navy in the Rev. War.

Sally Perkins is the only heir at law of Joshua Perkins, seaman in the Virginia Navy in the Rev. War. 1 Sept 1836. p. 63.

Richard J. Ayres is by the Court appointed guardian to George and Jane Satchell, infants of George Satchell, dec'd., and heirs of George and William Satchell. Richard J. Ayres is by the Court appointed guardian to Mary and James Satchell, infants of Zippa Satchell, dec'd. (and heirs of George and William Satchell). Ordered that Richard J. Ayres, guardian of George, Jane, Mary and James Satchell, infant heirs of George and William Satchell, soldiers in the Virginia Line in the Rev. War, sell, transfer and assign all certificates of military land scrip to which they may be entitled as heirs of said George and William Satchell. 26 Sept 1836. p. 70.

Ordered that Edmund B. Ayres, guardian of James Colonna alias Colona, and of Susan or Sukey Colonna alias Colony, infant heirs of George Satchell and William Satchell, soldier of the Virginia Line in the Rev. War, be authorized to sell, transfer and assign all certificates of military land scrip to which they may be entitled as heirs of said William and George Satchell. 26 Sept 1836. p. 71.

Samuel S. Stone is the grandson and only heir of David Gould, surgeon in the Virginia Line in the Rev. War. 26 Sept 1836. p. 73.

Zadock Bayly and Robert Bayly are the only heirs at law of Southey Bayly, seaman in the Virginia Navy in the Rev. War. 31 Oct 1836. p. 81.

Robert Bayly is the grandson and only heir at law of Robert Bayly, seaman in the Virginia Navy in the Rev. War. 31 Oct 1836. p. 81.

Leah Collins, child and only heir at law of Richard Pettigrew, states she is the dau. of said Richard Pettigrew; she is ca. 40 years of age; has frequently heard her father speak of his service on board the Accomack Galley in the Rev. War; he resided in Accomack until about 48 years ago when he removed to Kent Co., Delaware, where he died 5 Oct 1835. She has received a warrant for 100 acres of land for his services for three years. 29 Nov 1836. p. 93.

Molly, Nancy, John, Ephraim, James and William Wessells and Caty Russell are the only heirs at law of John Wessells, soldier in the 9th Va. Regt. in the Rev. War. 27 March 1837. p. 137.

Elizabeth Boniwell, orphan of McKeel Boniwell, one of the heirs of Thomas Boniwell, officer in the Virginia Navy in the Rev. War, chose Samuel C. White to be her guardian. 24 April 1837. p. 154.

Robert White, who was a midshipman in the Virginia Navy in the Rev. War, died intestate, leaving three children: Robert, Betsey and Margaret, all of whom died intestate. Robert the younger left three children: James H., Mary E. and Margaret I. White his only heirs at law. Betsey White left the following children: William J., Robert, Margaret, Betsey, Ralph, Sally, Mary and Charlotte Ross her only heirs at law. Said Margaret White left four children: Erastus, Eliza A., Mary and Louisa Hall, her only children and heirs at law. 30 April 1838. p. 315.

Charlotte Phillips, Louisa Small, wife of Gillett Small, Nancy Vernelson, Polly Hudson, William P. Thornton and Polly Thornton are the only heirs at law of Shadrack Chance who was a quarter master in the Virginia Navy in the Rev. War. 30 April 1838. p. 315.

Robert Russell, pensioner of the U.S., died 24 May 1837; Comfort Russell is his widow. 30 April 1838. p. 315.

Spencer Barnes is one of the heirs at law of Charles Copes, who served in the Rev. War instead of James Barnes whose name was heretofore certified to be one of the heirs of the said Charles Copes. 25 June 1838. p. 352.

William Bagwell is the only child and heir at law of Isaiah Bagwell, dec'd., who was the identical person named in a pension certificate now exhibited in Court and numbered 12891, and dated at the War Office of the U.S., 14 June 1833. Isaiah Bagwell died 8 Oct 1839. 25 Nov 1839. p. 617.

Charles Snead who was a captain in the 9th Va. Regt. on Continental Establishment in the Rev. War, died unmarried and childless before 1 Jan 1787. William Snead, formerly of Northampton Co., Virginia, was his eldest brother, and left two children, Mary and Anna; Mary Snead married John T. Elliott and died childless; Anna Snead married George F. Wilkins and died leaving one child, Mary Anne Wilkins. 27 Jan 1840. p. 645.

The order of this Court dated 31 Oct 1836, proving the heirs of Southy Bayly was an amendment of the order dated 29 July 1835, proving his said heirs, and the last order, dated 31 Oct 1836, contains the names of the true heirs of said Southy Bayly, seaman; the first order is erroneous. 24 Feb 1840. p. 657.

ORDERS 1840 - 1842

Peter Parker, son and one of the heirs at law of Richard Parker, who was a lieut. in the Virginia Navy in the Rev. War, died intestate; at his death he left no child or descendants of a child or parents living; he left his next of kin and heirs at law, two brothers, Levin Parker and John Parker and two nephews, Henry Stakes and James Stakes and one niece, Mary Ann Chandler, wife of Edward Chandler, the said Henry Stakes and James Stakes and Mary Ann Chandler being the only children of Nancy Stakes, formerly Nancy Parker, who was a sister of said Peter Parker. 31 March 1841. p. 221.

William Kennahorn was a pensioner of the U.S. at the rate of $8.00 per month, a resident of the said county and died therein on 30 Nov 1840; he left a widow, Delany Kennahorn. 31 March 1841. p. 221.

Leah Cameron is the only heir at law of Salathiel Simpson, dec'd., who was a master at arms in the Virginia Navy in the Rev. War. 31 May 1841. p. 246.

Elizabeth Corbin who was heretofore proved before this Court to be one of the heirs of Joseph, William and James Tunnell who served in the Virginia Navy in the Rev. War, has since died intestate, leaving three children: Edward and Robert Corbin and Milky Stant, wife of Edward Stant. Maria Marshall, another of the heirs of said Joseph, William and James Tunnell has also since died intestate and childless, leaving as her next of kin and heirs at law, Isaiah Tunnell, her only brother, and said Edward and Robert Corbin and Milkey Stant, who are the only children of her dec'd. sister, Elizabeth Corbin. 31 May 1841. p. 246.

It appears that the order heretofore made certifying that Betsey Justice, wife of Teackle Justice, is one of the heirs at law of Giles Taylor who served in the Virginia Navy in the Rev. War, is erroneous, and that Rosey Justice, wife of Teackle Justice should have been certified instead of Betsey Justice, and that said Giles Taylor died intestate. 26 July 1841. p. 281.

ORDERS 1842 - 1845

Scarborough Bloxom, who was a midshipman in the Virginia Navy in the Rev. War, was a pensioner of the U.S. at the time of his death in Oct 1836; he left a widow, Leah Bloxom who now resides in this co.; said Scarborough Bloxom married said Leah on or before 1790. 27 June 1842. p. 12.

William Henderson, a lieut. and capt. in the Rev. War on Continental Establishment, has since died intestate and without issue, leaving his brother Brittingham Henderson his only heir at law who has since died intestate leaving five children: Edward Henderson, James Henderson, John Henderson, Joseph Henderson and Nancy Henderson, his only heirs at law. Edward Henderson, James Henderson and John Henderson are still alive; Joseph Henderson died intestate leaving two children: Sebastian Henderson and Sally Henderson his only heirs at law. Nancy Henderson married Bundick Taylor and died intestate leaving four children: William, Sally, Henney and Mary Bundick her only heirs at law. 27 March 1843. p. 149.

John Walker, late of this co., died June 1796 leaving a will admitted 27 June 1796. During the Rev. War he was an officer in the Virginia Line; he left a widow, Elizabeth Walker, continuing his widow until her death on 8 Sept 1837. James Walker is her son and admr. 27 May 1844. p. 428. Elizabeth Walker left the following children: Sally Turlington, widow of John Turlington, John S. Walker, James Walker, Henry S. Walker and Ann Harmon; Ann Harmon died in 1843 leaving John Harmon, her husband, and the following children: William Harmon, John Harmon, Sally Willis, Anne Savage, Elizabeth Harmon and Catherine Harmon. Dorothy Walker who married Levi Hutchinson was a dau. of said John and Elizabeth Walker and died before her mother. 25 June 1844. p. 410.

Thomas Moore was a Rev. pensioner in the U.S. at the rate of $96.00 per annum, a resident of Accomack Co. at the time of his death on 31 Dec 1824, leaving a widow, Tabitha Moore, still his widow; she lives in the co. They were married 20 Sept 1844 before William P. Moore, Justice of the Peace for Accomack Co. (p. 524). 30 Sept 1844. p. 517.

John Rogers, an officer in the Rev. War, died in Accomack Co. more than 60 years ago; he left three sons: John, Major and Jacob and a dau. Tinney. John, Major and Tinney died leaving no issue. Jacob died leaving two daus.: Nancy and Molly Rogers. Nancy married Daniel Richardson and died leaving two daus: Polly and Sally. Molly Rogers married Richard Hutchinson and died leaving three children: Robert, Richard and Thomas. Polly Richardson married Richard Turner and died leaving two sons: George and Richard who are now living. Sally Richardson never married; is still living. 30 sep 1844. p. 517.

John Ashby, who was reputed to be an officer in the Rev. War, died intestate; his only heirs at law are Margaret Ashby and Sally Ashby (heirs of Smith Ashby), Sally Floyd's (heirs), Juliet Robbins, Elizabeth Savage, Lovey Ashby, Rachel Norworthy, Mary Fox, Ezekiel Ashby, Washbourn Ashby, Margaret Rayfield, David Ashby's heirs, Elizabeth Ashby, Norvilla Ames, Edward Ames, Georgianna Ames, John E. Ames,

Benjamin T. Ames, Mary Ames, Sally E. Mears and Elizabeth Mears. 29 Nov 1844. p. 532.

Comfort Russell who is inscribed on the pension list at Richmond, Virginia, who is the widow of Robert Russell, a soldier in the Rev. War, died in Accomack Co. 25 Nov 1844. p. 565.

ORDERS 1845 - 1848

John Moore was a sailing master in the Virginia Navy in the Rev. War. He died in Accomack co. early in the summer of 1798; his only dau. and child married Shadrick W. Outten formerly of Accomack, now of Elizabeth City, Virginia. 22 Feb 1846. p. 96.

By evidence of James Boggs and Thomas Underhill it appears that John Moore of Accomack Co. was a sailing master in the Virginia Navy in the Rev. War; that John Moore was a citizen of Virginia and died in Accomack Co. in the summer of 1790 [note that this differs with above paragraph.], and that the said John Moore left one child, Margaret Moore and that Margaret Moore married Shadrack W. Outten formerly of Accomack now of Elizabeth City Co., Virginia. It further appearing to the Court by said evidence of James Shelton that the said Shadrack W. Outten has now living by his marriage with said Margaret Moore the following children: Elizabeth, wife of John Baynes, Mary of legal age and unmarried, Purnell G. of legal age, Margaret, wife of Charles Bryan, Augustus, John and Martha Jane Outten (the last three of whom are under 21 years of age), and that the said Elizabeth Baynes, Mary Outten, Purnell G. Outten, Margaret Bryan, Augustus Outten, John Outten and Martha Jane Outten are the only heirs at law of the said John Moore who was a sailing master in the Virginia Navy in the Rev. War. 27 July 1846. p. 173.

It appears by evidence of Oliver Logan, that Robert White of Accomack Co., midshipman in the Virginia Navy in the Rev. War, died in Accomack Co. and left four children: Ralph who died and left no children; Robert who died intestate leaving three children: James H., Mary E. and Margaret J. White who died an infant of about 3 years of age; Elizabeth who married William Ross, both of whom are since dead leaving the following children: William, Robert, Margaret, Elizabeth, Sally, Mary and Charlotte, all of whom are yet living; Margaret who married Dixon Hall both of whom are since dead having the following children: Erastus, Eliza, Ann, Mary and Louisa Hall, all of whom are living - who are the only heirs at law of Robert White, Sr., who was a midshipman in the Virginia Navy in the Rev. War. 1 Sept 1846. p. 194.

ORDERS 1848 - 1851

Parker Copes, late a Rev. pensioner, died in this co. on 11 Jan 1849; Thomas P. Copes is his admr. 30 April 1849. p. 106.

Beverly Copes, dec'd., who was a midshipman in the Virginia Navy in the Rev. War. Admin. of his estate to John B. Ailworth.

John Snead, dec'd., who was a surgeon in the Virginia Navy in the Rev. War. Admin. of his estate to John B. Ailworth.

William Underhill, dec'd., who was captain in the Virginia Navy in the Rev. War. Admin. of his estate to John B. Ailworth. 27 Aug 1849. p. 171.

George Stewart, dec'd., who was a muster master, a pay master and a commissary general in the Virginia Navy in the Rev. War. Admin. of his estate to James S. Corbin. 27 Aug 1849. p. 170.

John Allen, dec'd., who was a captain in the Virginia Navy in the Rev. War. Admin. of his estate to Edmund R. Allen.

Hancock Simpson, dec'd, who was a coxman in the Virginia Navy in the Rev. War. Admin. of his estate to Littleton A. Hinman.

Admin. of the following estates appointed to John B. Ailworth:
John Cropper, Sr., dec'd., who was a captain in the Virginia Navy in the Rev. War.
Levin Bird, dec'd., who was a pilot in the Virginia Navy in the Rev. War.

Isaac Walters, dec'd., who was a boatswain's mate in the Virginia Navy in the Rev. War.
Levin Melson, dec'd., who was a coxswain's mate in the Virginia Navy in the Rev. War.
Robert Milliner, dec'd., who was a lieut. in the Virginia Navy in the Rev. War.

John Revell, dec'd., who was a gunners mate in the Virginia Navy in the Rev. War. Admin. de bonis non of his estate to Robert J. Poulson. Ordered that John Revell's will be admitted to probate on 28 April 1807. 25 June 1849. pp. 162-63.

John Murray is the heir at law of David Murray who was a sailing master in the Virginia Navy in the Rev. War. Said David Murray was at his death a citizen of this co. 24 Sept 1849. p. 178.

Robert Snead, dec'd., who was a surgeon in the Virginia Navy in the Rev. War. Admin. of his estate to John B. Ailworth.

John Pettigrew, dec'd., who was a lieut. in the Virginia Navy in the Rev. War. Admin. de bonis non with the will annexed, granted to John B. Ailworth. 24 Sept 1849. p. 178.

It appears from evidence by the oath of Jacob Jester, that Tabitha Moore, widow of Thomas Moore, pensioner of the U.S. at the rate of $80.00 per annum, was a resident of Accomack Co. and died in said co. ca. 6 Sept 1849; she left one child, Levi Moore. 31 Dec 1849. p. 249.

John Berry Hickman, who made a declaration before this Court on 28 Aug 1832, and John Berry, Sr., whose will was admitted to probate 31 July 1843, were one and the same person, and he was in the habit of indiscriminately signing his name as John Berry or John Berry Hickman. It is certified that the following children of John Berry Hickman or John Berry, Sr., are now living: Tinney Mears (formerly Tinney Berry), William P. Berry, Samuel Berry, Charles Berry and Ann Lewis (formerly Ann Berry). 30 Sept 1850. p. 403.

Bowdoin Snead was a pensioner of the U.S. at the rate of $80.00 per annum; he was a resident of Accomack Co. and died in the said co. ca. 1 July 1841; he left a widow now living whose name is Mary Snead; the pension certificate has been lost.

Edmund Read was a pensioner of the U.S. at the rate of $80.00 per annum; he was a resident of the state of Virginia and died in Accomack Co. ca. 23 Dec 1836; he left two children: Maria Scarburgh and Mary H. Higgins; the pension certificate has been lost.

Jonathan Phillips died in 1835 leaving a widow, Comfort Phillips, now living; they were married in prior to 1794.

Daniel Bull was a pensioner of the U.S. at the rate of $80.00 per year; he resided in Accomack Co.; he died in said co. ca. April 1835 leaving one child, Eliza Taylor, formerly Eliza Bull; pension certificate has been lost.

John Phillips died 8 or 9 Oct 1849; William P. Moore, Jr. is exr.

Richard Wimbrough, Rev. soldier, died 25 June 1845; he left the following children: Mary Wimbrough and Rachel Wimbrough.

James Davis ---, died last day of Jan 1850 and left the following children: Noah Davis, Henry Davis and Betsy Hall, formerly Betsy Davis. 28 Oct 1850. pp. 411-12.

Sarah C. Chase, wife of Moses B. Chase (who now resides in Cambridge, Mass.) is the dau. of Col. Levin Joynes, dec'd., formerly of this co. who as a colonel in the Virginia Line in the Rev. War. She is the same Sarah mentioned as his dau. in the codicil to his will; Ann Smith Joynes, another dau. of said Levin Joynes named in the codicil to his will died in New Hampshire in 1843; Julianna L. Chase named in her [?] will is upwards of 21 years of age; James M. Chase named in her [?] will, will be 21 years of age on 7 Dec 1850; Reginald H., Virginia M. and Sarah J. Chase mentioned in said will are minors. 25 Nov 1850. p. 417.

John Parkes who filed a declaration for a pension in Accomack Co. in 1832 for his services in the Rev. War, died 22 March 1841, leaving his son John Parkes his exr., and leaving a widow, Ann Parks who died on 20 March 184- leaving John Parkes, Tabitha Taylor and Nancy Killman her only children and heirs at law. 25 Nov 1850. p. 423.

Hillary Mears, a soldier of the Rev. War, died ca. 1 April 1836, leaving no widow but leaving the following children: William B. Mears, Jesse Mears, Nancy Mears who married John Turlington, George Mears and Elizabeth Mears. Since his death the following have died: Nancy Turlington, wife of said John Turlington, who left the following children: William T. Turlington and Nathaniel Turlington who are 21 years of age and upwards, Elizabeth A. Turlington and John H. Turlington, minors; Peter Turlington is their guardian. William B. Mears died leaving children: David P. Mears who is 21 years or older, Jesse Mears and Thomas Mears who are minors. George H. Bell is admr. of the estate of Hillary Mears. 30 Dec 1850. p. 432.

Housten Kellam was a soldier in the Rev. War; he died 13 Jan 1847 leaving a widow, Elizabeth Kallam who remains his widow. 30 Dec 1850. p. 432.

William Elliott, Rev. soldier, was a resident of this co. and died ca. 23 Sept 1836 leaving a widow, Anxell Elliott; she died 7 Oct 1841 leaving one child, Anzell Wallace who still survives. William Elliott and Anzell married 10 Dec 1781. 30 Dec 1850. p. 433.

Adam Mason, Rev. soldier, was a resident of this co.; he died in this co. ca. 15 Nov 1835 leaving no widow, but leaving one child, William Mason who is now living in the co.

Jacob Sparrow, Rev. soldier, lived in this co. and died ca. 31 Dec 1842. He left one child, Samuel Sparrow and no widow.

Thomas Lewis, Rev. soldier, is still alive and applies on 29 Aug 1832 to obtain benefits under the act of 7 June 1832.

Susan Chandler, widow of Littleton Chandler, was a widow of Littleton Chandler; was a resident of this co.; died in this co. 22 April 1849 leaving the following children: Nancy Chandler, Margaret E. Chandler and Eliza Chandler. Susan Chandler and Littleton Chandler married 7 Sept 1778. 30 Dec 1850. pp. 435-36.

William Harrison was a resident of Accomack Co.; died in this co. ca. 15 Nov 1834 leaving a widow, Molly Harrison, who is still alive. 27 Jan 1851. p. 448.

Levin Hyslop was a pensioner of the Rev.; he died ca. 27 April 1835 leaving a widow, Susan, who died ca. 16 Sept 1848. She left two children: Elizabeth Hutchinson, formerly Elizabeth Davis and James Hyslop, her only heirs at law. 27 Jan 1851. p. 450.

John Phillips died ca. 9 Oct 1848 leaving no widow; William P. Moores, Senr. is his exr.; his heirs are Levin W. Phillips, Hetty Bradford and Susan Phillips. 24 Feb 1851. p. 458.

Rosa Harmon and Sina Harmon declared that they are the children and heirs at law of John Harmon, dec'd., who served as a soldier during the Rev. War; they claim the arrears of pension now due on account of the said services of said John Harmon, dec'd. They believe a pension has issued to Edward O. Finey and Garrison Burton, exrs. of said John Harmon, dec'd. They further declare that such certificate issued without their consent or approbation and contrary to their wishes; they desire a new certificate of pension to issue directly to themselves; and they appoint Henry A. Wise their attorney. 24 Feb 1851. p. 458.

John Drummond, Senr., of Accomack Co., who applied for a pension, died June 1833 leaving a widow who is now dead; Nancy Drummond, Patience Marshall and Sophia White are his only surviving children and heirs at law. 24 Feb 1851. p. 458.

James Drummond who was a lieut., died in the Rev. War intestate, leaving no children nor descendants of children but leaving three brothers and two sisters: John Drummond (his eldest bother), Stephen Drummond, William Drummond, Comfort Drummond and Sophia Drummond, his only heirs at law. John Drummond (eldest brother of James) died many years ago intestate, leaving six children: John P. Drummond, Sally Drummond, Tabitha Drummond, Patience Marshall, Nancy Drummond and Sophia White his only children and heirs at law. John P. Drummond died intestate leaving Elizabeth Mears, Tabitha Grant, Enos Drummond, Scipio Drummond, John Drummond and Nancy Drummond his only children and heirs at law. Sally Drummond (dau. of John) died intestate leaving John R. Drummond, Levin J. Drummond and Oliver P. Drummond her only children and heirs at law. Tabitha Drummond (dau. of John) also died intestate leaving Levin Lewis and Thomas Lewis her only children and heirs at law. Stephen Drummond (brother of James) died intestate leaving Hill Drummond, James Drummond, Ketturah Weston and Elizabeth Middleton, wife of William Middleton, his only children and heirs at law. William Drummond (brother of James) died intestate leaving Nancy Drummond, Caty Drummond, William S. Drummond and Richard Drummond his only children and heirs at law. Comfort Drummond (sister of James) died intestate leaving Spencer Drummond, Sally Corbin, William Drummond, John C. Drummond and Noah Drummond her only children and heirs at law. Sophia Drummond (sister of James) died intestate leaving Henry Hall her grandson, her only heir at law. 24 Feb 1851. p. 459.

Deposition of Isaac D. Robins, age 63, states he was acquainted with Isma Fletcher (Rev. soldier) for the last 50 odd years and believes he served in said war. He was acquainted with Fletcher's wife who died a few weeks before his Fletcher's death on 7 Oct 1836. Isma Fletcher left the following children: Isma Fletcher, Tinny Fletcher, Edward Fletcher and Jessee Fletcher his only surviving children and heirs at law. Given 14 March 1851 before William P. Moore, Jr., J.P. 31 March 1851. p. 472.

Thomas Robins was a resident of this co. and died in the co. ca. 1836 leaving no widow, and the following children now living: Isaac D. Robins, George W. Robins, Nancy Lewis, Elizabeth Elliott, Malinda Downs and Juliet Darby. 31 March 1851. p. 473.

ORDERS 1851 - 1854

Thomas Lewis was a soldier in the Rev. War; he died 2 March 1851 leaving a widow, Sarah Lewis who remains his widow.

James Marshall of "Sykes Island' to whom was recently granted a pension, was a resident of this co. and died in said co. ca. 9 Jan 1851 leaving a widow, Patience Marshall who is still living.

William Welbourn, Sr., resident in Accomack Co., died in this co. between 15 and 20 Oct 1839. There is no widow living; he left the following children: Susan Wallop, Hester Marshall, Margaret Marshall, Eliza Rowley, John D. Welborn, Peter Welbourn and William Welbourn.

Maddox Fisher was a resident of this co. and died in this co. 31 March 1834; he left a widow who died 18 July 1843; they left no children. Peter F. Brown is admr. of Maddox Fisher's estate.

Samuel Marshall whose heirs claim a pension for his services as a soldier in the Rev. War, lived on Saxis Island in Accomack Co. and died ca. 15 Feb 1835 leaving the following children: Washington Marshall, Milly Lewis and Elizabeth Tyler. 28 April 1851. pp. 4-5.

Jacob Edwards was a pensioner of the U.S.; he resided in this co. until 1834 when he emigrated to North Carolina; it appears by affidavit of J. J. W. Powell, the attending physician and Mr. P. Edwards, that he died in Edgecomb Co., NC, ca. 4 Oct 1837 leaving one child, John B. Edwards in that state and one child Sally Gardner formerly Sally Edwards in this state, and no widow. 28 April 1851. p. 13.

Susan Chandler, widow of Littleton Chandler, resided in Accomack Co. and died in the same co. on 22 April 1849 leaving the following children: Nancy Chandler, Margaret E. Chandler and Eliza Chandler. On 28 April 1851 P. F. Brown, admr. of Susan Chandler made a declaration in behalf of the children. He stated the records show Littleton Chandler was a private in the companies of Capt. Joynes and Capt. George Oldham, attached to the regiment commanded by Col. Southy Simpson. Susan Chandler and Littleton Chandler married 7 Sept 1778. Littleton Chandler died 4 July 1832. 28 April 1851. p. 14.

Robert Corbin, son of Robert Corbin, stated that he had been informed by Robert Chase, a Rev. pensioner, and others in the neighborhood, that his father, Robert Corbin, performed military duty in the Rev. War; that he enrolled in a company of militia commanded by Capt. Jesse Dickerson in 1778 or 79 under Col. Simpson. That kept guard at "Houldings Creek" and other places on the sea and bay side. Robert Chase said he served with him on guard and he believes that Corbin served two years or more. His father, Robert Corbin, was born in Accomack Co. 3 Feb 1764 and died at age 79. Declaration made in behalf of the children of Robert Corbin, dec'd. 30 June 1851. p. 51.

Declaration of Teackle Justice, son of Richard Justice, Rev. soldier, in order to obtain benefits for the children of Richard Justice. It appears by the affidavit of Robert Chase, Rev. soldier and pensioner, who lived nearly all his life in the neighborhood of Richard Justice, that he performed military duty in the Rev. War. He was enrolled in a company of militia commanded by Capt. William Justice; served with him in keeping guard at Block House on Folly Creek and says that Capt. William Justice's company was actively engaged in keeping guard, marches, &c.; he is satisfied that his father was on duty at various times for more than two years. He did not assert his claim to a pension in his lifetime because the claims of Robert Chase and Richard Wimbrough who served with him had been rejected. He was born in Accomack Co. in 1749 and died at age 102. 30 June 1851. p. 52.

William Tunnell who served in the Virginia Navy in the Rev. War, mentioned in an order of the Court on 28 July 1835 in which Isaiah Tunnell, Elizabeth Corbin and Maria Marshall are proved to be the only heirs at law of William Tunnell - that Maria Marshall has since died intestate and without issue; Elizabeth Corbin has also died leaving Robert Corbin, Edward Corbin and Milcah Stant, wife of Edward Stant as her only children and heirs at law. 30 June 1851. p. 55.

Richard Justice, whose services in the Rev. War were declared by his son, died ca. 17 May 1850, leaving no widow but the following children: Teackle Justice, Samuel Justice and Margaret Justice. 28 July 1851. p. 64.

Darmone Darby, dec'd., left at his death the following children: Peggy and Betsy Darby. Peggy Darby died leaving two children: Walter W. Darby and Lovey Darby, now Lovey Only, both of whom are now living. The said Betsy Darby, later Betsy Lewis, died leaving two children: Edward and Ann Lewis, now Ann Pitts, both of whom are now living. 26 Aug 1851. p. 76.

Robert Corbin who served in the Rev. War, a resident of this co., died in the co. ca. 15 Nov 1843 leaving no widow but the following children: Milcah Stant, Edward and Robert Corbin. 26 Aug 1851. p. 76.

Declaration of Elizabeth Summers, widow of Richard Summers, dec'd. She states she (former name was Elizabeth Lewis) married Richard Summers and they lived as husband and wife until his death on 7 July past. She heard him speak of his services in the militia during the War; his brother, Horsey Summers, served with him. Her husband served, she believes, over two years. Her husband lived on the Virginia (Accomack Co.)/Maryland line during the Rev. War on the Maryland side and crossed over into Accomack and was married there by Rev. George H. Ewell and resided there until he died, in his 91st year. Certificate from Rev. Ewell, acquainted with Richard Summers for at least 60 years. 29 Sept 1851. p. 109.

Declaration of Horsey Summers, age 89. He states he served in the militia of Somerset Co., Maryland from the time he was in his 15th year of age. They were frequently called out to keep guard and suppress the tories, who were frequently trying to discourage them by telling them that "the British would take us and if they did we should all be hung." On one occasion Col. Southy Simpson's Company of militia was ordered from the Virginia side to assist us in destroying the "Tory Camp" where the tories all collected and were furnished with arms from the British, and in the engagement in which he took part the tories were routed and had to take to the British ships which were then lying in sight in Tangier harbour to blockade the Pocomoke Sound. Col. Gunbey had command of the militia. He said that he was a private in the various companies of Henry Miles, then Capt. Starling and last Capt. John Cox, and performed service and kept guard at Apes hold, Summers Cove and Miles Gum, which was the general place of meeting at which place he swore allegiance to his country and against the King of Great Britain. He recollects his Capt. Cox told his men to put their names to that paper or they deserved kicking out of the company. He was in service more than two years, off from all other employment. He was born in Somerset Co., Maryland on the Virginia line and shortly after the close of the war he crossed over onto the Virginia side into Accomack Co. where he married and has resided ever since. 29 Sept 1851. p. 110.

Benjamin Colonna, Rev. pensioner, was a resident of this co. and died in the co. 2 July 1851 leaving no widow but the following children: John W. Colonna, Abel B. Colonna, Major D. Colonna, Benjamin S. Colonna and Mary Doughty. John W. Colonna and Benjamin S. Colonna are his exrs. 27 Oct 1851. p. 113.

William Watson was a resident of this co. and died in this co. ca. 26 Sept 1840 leaving no widow but the following children: Tabitha Mason, Kessey Pearson, Sally Kellam and James Watson. William P. Moore, Jr. is his admr. 27 Oct 1851. p. 115.

Custis Bull, Rev. pensioner, was a resident of this co. and died in the co. on 1 Sept 1851 leaving no widow but the following children: Rosey, Nancy, Polly, Charles, Betsey. His son Charles Bull is his admr. 27 Oct 1851. p. 115.

John Drummond (brother of James Drummond who was reputed to be a Rev. officer) died many years ago, intestate, leaving John P. Drummond, Sally Drummond, Tabitha Drummond, Nancy Drummond, Sophia White and Patience Marshall his only children and heirs at law. Nancy Drummond, Sophia White and Patience Marshall are still living. John P. Drummond, son of John, died intestate leaving Elizabeth Mears, Tabitha Grant, Nancy Drummond, John Drummond, Scipio Drummond and Enos Drummond his only children and heirs at law. Sally Drummond, dau. of John, died intestate leaving John R. Drummond, Levin J. Drummond and Oliver Drummond her only children and heirs at law. Tabitha Drummond married John Lewis and died intestate leaving Thomas D. Lewis, Levin D. Lewis and Sarah Lewis her only children and heirs at law. Sarah Lewis, dau. of Tabitha, married John Lewis who died intestate, and left Tabitha Johnson her only heir at law. 26 Jan 1852. p. 155.

Stephen Warrington who was reputed to have served in the Rev. War, died many years ago leaving the following children his only heirs at law: George Warrington, Samuel Warrington, Peggy Warrington, Sally Warrington, Nancy Warrington, Smith Warrington and Thomas Warrington. Nancy Warrington (now Nancy Smith) and Thomas Warrington are still living. Sally Warrington married William Parson and is dead. Samuel and George Warrington died intestate leaving no children nor descendants of children. John K. Warrington died leaving Lovey Warrington, now Lovey Ames, John T. Warrington and Sally Warrington (now Sally Belote) his only children and heirs at law. Peggy Warrington married William Whitehead and died intestate leaving John Whitehead, William Whitehead and Edward Whitehead her only children and heirs at law. 17 Jan 1852. p. 155.

Edward Henderson, James Henderson, John Henderson, Joseph Henderson and Nancy Henderson who on 27 March 1843 were proved in this Court to be heirs of Brittingham Henderson, who was the only heir at law of Capt. William Henderson, who served in the Rev. War, have since died intestate except Edward who is still living. James Henderson, son of Brittingham, died leaving no child nor descendant of children. John Henderson, son of Brittingham, died leaving two children who are his only heirs: Samuel and Milly Henderson. Joseph Henderson, son of Brittingham, died leaving two children, Sebastian Henderson and Sally Henderson, his only children and heirs at law. Nancy Henderson, dau. of Brittingham, married Bundick Taylor and died leaving William Taylor, Sally Taylor, Henny Taylor and Mary Taylor her only children and heirs at law. Said Sally and Mary have since died under age and in infancy, leaving their brother William and sister Henny Taylor the only heirs at law of the said Nancy Taylor, formerly Nancy Henderson. In the former order of this Court it referred to the above heirs of Nancy Taylor formerly Nancy Henderson, viz: William, Sally, Henny and Mary should by Taylor and not Bundick. 17 Jan 1852. p. 156.

James S. Corbin, Mary Jane Taylor, formerly Mary Jane Corbin and Sarah Ann Metz, formerly Sarah Ann Corbin, are the only heirs at law of George Stewart who was a muster master, pay master and purchasing commissary to the Accomac Dilligence Galleys in the Virginia Navy in the Rev. War. George Stewart died intestate. 23 Feb 1852. p. 163.

Since the order certifying the heirs of Robert White, dec'd., who was a midshipman in the Virginia Navy rendered on 29 Nov 1847, the following named heirs of said Robert White, dec'd., named in the said order, have died and married as follows: Elizabeth Ross has married Jolly and since died leaving an infant who is also dead; Tully Joseph died an infant; Charlotte Ross married Robert Lamden and is still living; Margaret Ross married John Bennett and is still living; Mary Hall married Thomas Holland and is sill living; Louisa Hall married Elijah Maddox and is still living. 27 Dec 1852. p. 337.

Hetty Trader, one of the heirs of Robert Bayly is now the wife of Henry Davis. Robert and Henry Bayly are still living; Polly died intestate and without issue; Betsy Bayly and Betsy Wessells are still living. 28 Feb 1853. p. 356.

William Thornton, one of the heirs of Jabez Taylor, died intestate leaving his son William Thornton his only heir at law. William Thornton died intestate leaving his two sons Charles Thornton and John Thornton his only children and heirs at law to whom James T. Palmer has been appointed guardian. 28 Feb 1853. p. 356.

Spencer Lewis of Accomack Co., age ca. 90 years, who served in the Rev. War, said that he was acquainted with Thomas Nelson who was one of the militiamen in the Rev. War and has been considered to be 100 years old. Revd. George H. Ewell, age 73, certifies that he understood from his father who served in the War (and many others) that said Thomas Nelson was one of the militia of Accomack and served in the Rev. War and has no doubt that Nelson is over 100 years of age. 15 Feb 1853. Recorded 28 Feb 1853. p. 358.

Declaration of Sabra Waples, age 62, who states she is a widow of Samuel Waples who was a lieut., 9th Regt. Virginia Line; that her husband was a pensioner under Act of May 15, 1828 at the rate of $320.00 per annum, paid at the Agency in Richmond, Virginia. She married Samuel Waples 22 Aug 1822; he died 11 Aug 1834. She is now a widow. 25 April 1853. p. 398.

Elkanah Andrews was a Rev. pensioner of the U.S. at the rate of $96.00 per annum; he died 16 Sept 1844, leaving Samuel Andrews his only child. 1 June 1853. p. 415.

Patience Marshall, widow of James Marshall, died 11 Aug 1853 leaving the following children: Zachariah Marshall and Tiffany Linton. 31 Oct 1853. p. 487.

Elizabeth Hutchinson, age 66, states she is the widow of George Snead, dec'd, who was a private in the continental line of Virginia and served three years in a company and regiment unknown to her; many years ago he was allowed bounty land for his services. He resided in Accomack Co. until he died. She married George Snead 10 Jan 1810; he died 24 Dec 1816. She married Edmd. Hutchinson 16 Jan 1817; he died 10 Jan 1828. She is now a widow. 31 Oct 1853. p. 489.

John K. Warrington (one of the children of Stephen Warrington, who served in the Rev. War) died leaving John T. Warrington, Lovey C. Charnock and Sally Belote his only children and heirs at law. Lovey C. Charnock is now Lovey C. Ames; John T. Warrington has died intestate leaving the following children: Emily S. Warrington, John R. Warrington and William A. Warrington who are minors. 26 Dec 1853. p. 513.

Leah Cameron who was the only heir of Salathiel Sampson, master at arms in the Virginia Navy, has died since the former order of this Court proving the heirship of said Salathiel Simpson; Ann B. and Sarah L. Cameron are the only living children and heirs at law of said Leah Cameron who died intestate. 26 Dec 1853. p. 516.

Robert Chase of Accomack Co. a Rev. pensioner died in said co. 19 Nov 1853, leaving a widow named Sally Chase who is still living his widow; they lived together as husband and wife upwards of 40 years and had four or five children born during that time; they were always regarded as husband and wife by the community. 26 Dec 1853. p. 520.

Elizabeth Dunton, late Elizabeth Willis, who was certified on 27 Sept 1831, to be one of the heirs at law of David and James Ashby, is entitled in right of her mother to 1/3 of the land bounty scrip issued for the services of said David and James Ashby; her mother died intestate. 27 Feb 1854. p. 545.

ORDERS 1854 - 1857

Mrs. Susan Hyslop, an applicant for a Rev. pension as the widow of Levin Hyslop, who was a pensioner, died in said co. on 16 Sept 1848; James Hyslop of said co. is the only surviving child of said Levin and Susan Hyslop who is now living. Said Susan and Levin Hyslop married in 1798; Levin Hyslop died in 1835. 26 June 1854. p. 65.

Whereas in a former order certifying the children of Margaret, dau. of Robert White, midshipman, it was certified that Margaret Hall left five children: Erastus, Eliza, Anne, Mary and Louisa, it is corrected that there were four children: Erastus, Eliza Anne (one person), Mary and Louisa. 26 June 1854. p. 67.

Nancy Bayly, widow of Robert Bayly, reputed soldier in the Rev. War, died Aug 1846; Elizabeth Wessells is her only living child. 29 Jan 1855. p. 168.

Sally Chase, a pensioner of the U.S., died 11 Sept 1855 leaving the following children: Robert Chase, Sally Killman, Natia Marshall and Jane Trader. 25 Feb 1856. p. 364.

Sabra P. Waples was a pensioner of the U.S. at the rate of $320.00 per annum; was a resident of Accomack Co.; died in said co. 23 Dec 1856 leaving the following children: Sarah T. Waples, Edward B. Waples, Martha W. Waples and Mary D. Robertson (formerly Waples), widow of William Robertson. 28 April 1857. p. 608.

ORDERS 1857 - 1860

Elizabeth Mears, who was proven in the Court on 29 July 1855 to be an heir at law of Charles Copes, dec'd, soldier in the Rev. War, died ca. 1843 intestate, leaving Henry Copes her child and only heir; Sally Copes who was also proved to be one of the heirs at law of said Charles Copes, died ca. 1838 intestate, leaving Henry Copes her child and Savage Copes and Elizabeth Copes her grandchildren and only heirs at law; James Barnes who was also proved to be one of the heirs at law of said Charles Copes dec'd., died ca. 1836 intestate and has no issue living. Elizabeth Mears, Henry Copes, Savage Copes and Elizabeth Copes are the only heirs at law of Charles Copes, dec'd. 29 March 1858. p. 153.

Sally Chase, a pensioner of the U.S. and to whom bounty land warrant no. 27, 629, dated 24 May 1856 for 160 acres was granted as the widow of Robert Chase, a private in the Rev. War, died in this co. intestate previous to the date of the said warrant; she left the following and only children and heirs: Jinny Trader (born Chase), wife of Valentine Trader, Natia Marshall (born Chase), widow of Isaac Marshall, Polly Killman (born Chase), widow of James Killman, Robert Chase and Susan Ross (born Chase), widow of Ezekiel Ross. Since the death of said Sally Chase, Robert Chase and Susan Ross have died; Susan left Levin T. Ross her only child and heir at law; Robert Chase left the following children and heirs at law: Teackle Chase, Alsivada Chase, Sally Chase, Mary, wife of James Stant, Elizabeth, wife of Raymond Trader, Comfort Chase, Kendal Chase, Brunetta Chase and Nancy Chase. 30 May 1859. p. 449.

John P. Drummond, late a resident of this co. and who is reputed to be a prosecutor of Rev. land claims, died intestate in 1840, leaving four children his only heirs at law: Tabitha J. Drummond, wife of Edward S. Grant, John Richard Drummond and Nancy Drummond, all of whom are now living, and Elizabeth H. Drummond who married Thomas Mears who has since died leaving three children: Teagle Mears, John W. Mears and Sarah A. Mears, all of whom are living, for whom Edward S. Grant is guardian. 30 Jan 1860. p. 603.

MINUTE BOOK 1771-1777

The Declaration of Independence of the Thirteen United States of North America was proclaimed at the Door of the Courthouse, and agreeable to a Resolve of the honorable Convention of this State the Magistrates proceeded to take the Oath of fidelity to the State & the Oath of Office in order to take upon them the administration of Justice in the said County of Northampton.

John Stratton, Michl. Christian, John Harmanson, Nathaniel Lytt Savage, John Wilkins (O.P.), Littleton Savage, John Robins & Henry Guy, Gentlemen, named in the last commission of the peace took the Oaths to the State & the Oaths of that office agreeable to the said Ordinance. 13 August, 1776. p. 228.

The Court recommends Shadrack Ames to be Capt. of the Militia in the room of John Blair who is promoted, also Obedience Johnson to be Lieutenant in the room of the said (no name-S.N.) and Caleb Smith to be Ensign in the room of the said Obedience. 9 Oct. 1776. p. 230.

Recommended: Edmund Glanville to be Capt. of the new company of Militia to be raised, Drury Stith Lieut. and Michl. Christian Junr. to be Ensign. 9 Oct. p. 231.

Eyre Stockley Manager of a private Saltworks the property of Mr. John Stratton, made Oath that he made at the said Works on the 20th of July till the 6th of November inst. two hundred bushels of Salt, ordered therefore that the same be certified to the Treasurer to entitle the said Stratton to the bounty allowed by the Ordinance of Convention. 12 Nov. 1776. p. 231.

Recommended: John Kendall, Jr., Gentleman, to be appointed Lieut: to the Company of Militia whereof Thos. Parsons is Capt. & Mr. Bowdoin Kendall to be Ensign. 14 Jan 1777. p. 248

Henry Guy, Jr. to be Capt. of the Militia of the Company late Commanded by Capt. Wm. Floyd & John Bowdoin to be Lieut: & Ralph Dixon Ensign.

Thos. Evans to be Ensign of Capt. Rickards Dunton's Company.

Harrison Thomas to be Ensign in Capt. Ames' Company.

Peter Dickinson to be Capt. Mapp's Ensign.

82   *NORTHAMPTON COUNTY*

Edmund Glanville Capt. of the Militia, Drury Stith Lieut: & Michael Christian Junr. Ensign qualified to their Comms.

Henry Guy Junr, Capt; John Bowdoin, Lieut; John Kendall Junr, Lieut; Bowdoin Kendall, Ensign; Luke Heath, Ensign & Ralph Dixon Ensign severally qualified to their Commissions 11 Feb. 1777. p. 238.

"The Court were of opinion in the present Contest of America &c. to call on the following persons to take the Oath of fidelity to America (to wit) Dr. Fulwell, Samuel Atchison, Thos. Atchison, James Imry, John Begg, James Ingram, James Taylor, James Tait, Walter Hyslop, Francis Miller, William Barber and Nathl. Stevenson, and the said Fulwell, Sam: and Tho: Atchison and John Begg and Francis Miller and Walter Hyslop and John Hamilton appeared and refused to take the said Oath, and the said James Tait also appeared and prayed, and had leave granted him to consider thereof till tomorrow, and the said Francis Miller also declared that being a Custom house Officer in the late Government under the Crown of Great Britain, he could not take the said Oath as it would deprive him of his Salary &c. relating to his said Office if he should return to Great Britain, and the said Ingram not appearing ordered that he be summoned to appear here tomorrow, and the said James Taylor and Nathl. Stevenson took the said Oath, the said Taylor being presented by Dr Fulwell and not suspected by the Court he having before taken the said Oath as prosecutor for the Commonwealth." 11 Mar. 1777. p. 241.

Shadrack Ames, Captain; Obedience Johnson, Lieut: & Harrison Thomas, Ensign, severally took the Oaths to be true to the Commonwealth & the Oath of officers of the Militia. 8 Apr. 1777 -p. 243

Hillary Stringer is appointed Ensign to Captain Glanville's Company. 10 June 1777. p. 250.

MINUTE BOOK 1777 - 1783
Recommendations: Hezekiah Pitts to be 2nd lieut. of Capt. Thomas Fisher's Company.

Peter Dickerson 2nd lieut. & Elias Waterfield Ensign of Capt. John Mapp's Company, also Bowdoin Kendall 2nd lieut. & Benjamin Warren Ensign of Capt. Parsons' Company.

Thomas Evans 2nd lieut: and Wm. Waterfield to be Ensign of Capt. Rickards Dunton's Company.

Harrison Thomas, 2nd lieut. and John Robins Junr. to be ensign of Capt. Ames' company.

Ralph Dixon 1st Lieut: and Wm. Gibb to be 2nd Lieut: & Richard Street Ensign of Capt: Guy's Company.

Hillary Stringer 2nd Lieut: & Stephen Sampson Ensign of Capt. Glanvill's Company.

Mr. Daniel R. Hall to be Captain of a new Company to be raised, George Savage 1st lieut: Henry Wilkins 2nd lieut: and Wm. Trower ensign. 12 Aug. 1777. p. 7.

Recommendations:

Hillary Stringer to be 1st Lieut.; Stephen Sampson 2nd Lieut.; & Thos. Nottingham Junr. Ensign of Capt. Glanvill's Company. 9 Sept. 1777. p. 9.

Hillary Stringer 1st Lieut: & Stephen Sampson 2nd Lieut and Thomas Nottingham Junr. Ensign of Capt. Glanvill's Company, Daniel Raales Hall Capt, Henry Wilkins 1st Lieut:, William Trower 2nd Lieut: and Jonathan Stott 1st Lieut: of Capt. Dunton's Company and William Waterfield Ensign, Elias Waterfield Ensign of Capt. Mapp's Company, William Gibb 2nd Lieut: of Capt. Guy's Company, Bowdoin Kendall 2nd Lieut: of Capt. Parson's Company took the Oath of Office.

John Thos. to be Capt. of a new Company & Harrison Thomas 1st Lieut: Thos. Fisher 2nd Lieut: and Caleb Fisher Ensign.

John Robins late Ensign of Capt. Ames' Company to be 2nd Lieut: of the said Company and Wm. Fisher Ensign.

Ralph Dixon 1st Lieut of Capt. Guy's Company: Will: Trower 2nd Lieut: of Capt. Hall's Co: & Hezekiah Pitts 2nd Lieut: of Capt. Fisher's Company.

John Thomas Captain of a new Company.

Harrison Thomas 1st Lieut: of Capt. Thomas' Company.

Thos. Fisher Senr 2nd Lieut: of the said Company.

Robert Trower Ensign of Capt. Hall's Company took the oath of Office. 14 Oct. 1777. p. 10.

Examination of Robert Pierson lately cast away on Hog Island in this County, it appearing by his confession that the said Robert belonged to the schooner Molly of the British Fleet bound from Chesapeake Bay to New York, and was cast away by stress of Weather. Ordered said Robert be delivered to Colo. Gish by the Sheriff as a prisoner of War. 15 Oct. 1777. p. 11.

Appointed: Henry Wilkins Gent., appointed 1st Lieut: of Capt. Hall's

Company; took the Oath of fidelity to the Commonwealth and the Oath of the said office.

Peter Dickerson, Gent., appointed 2nd Lieut. of Capt. Mapp's Company; took the Oath of fidelity to the Commonwealth and the Oath of his said office. 12 Nov. 1777. p. 13.

Recommended: John Wilkins to be County Lieut: on the room of John Burton who resigned, Isaac Avery to be Colo. in the room of John Wilkins who's promoted, Maj: John Robins to be Lieut Colo. in the room of Colo. Avery, Thomas Fisher eldest Capt. to be Major in the room of Maj: John Robins. John Darby to be Capt. of Thomas Fisher's Company. Hezekiah Pitts to be 1st Lieut: in the room of the said John Darby, Luke Heath 2nd Lieut: in the said Company. William Downing to be Ensign of the said Company. John Kendall Junr. to be Capt. in the room of Thomas Parsons who resigned. Bowdoin Kendall 1st Lieut: Benjamin Warren 2nd Lieut: and John Elliott to be Ensign to the said Company. Ralph Dixon Capt. in the room of Henry Guy who resigned, Richard Street 1st Lieut: Ezekiel McCready 2nd Lieut: and Samuel Johnson Ensign to the said Company. Henry Wilkins Capt. in the room of Daniel R. Hall who resigned, William Trower 1st Lieut: Robert Trower 2nd Lieut:, and John Stratton Junr. Ensign to the said Company, Peter Dickerson to be 1st Lieut: of Capt. Mapp's Company in the room of Charles Carpenter who resigned, Elias Waterfield 2nd Lieut: and Richard Nottingham Ensign.

Harrison Thomas to be Capt. in the room of John Thomas who resigned, Thomas Fisher Senr 1st Lieut: Caleb Fisher 2nd Lieut and Jonathan Matthews Ensign to the said Company. 14 Apr. 1778. pp. 45-46-47.

John Wilkins County Lieut; Isaac Avery, Colo; John Robins Lieut: Colo; Thomas Fisher Junr. Major; John Kendall Junr. Capt; Bowdoin Kendall 1st Lieut: and Richard Nottingham 2nd Lieut: took the Oaths of Fidelity to the Commonwealth. 15 Apr. 1778. p. 49.

Richard Nottingham 1st Lieut:, Benjamin Dunton 2nd Lieut: and Seth Powell Ensign to Capt. Mapp's Company. 12 May 1778. p. 51.

Qualified: Captains John Darby, Harrison Thomas & Ralph Dixon & Lieut: Wm. Trower qualified to the Commissions. 12 May 1778. p. 54.
Richard Street 1st Lieut: to Capt. Dixon's Company. 12 May 1778. p. 45.

Recommended: Isaac Avery to be County Lieut: in the room of John

Wilkins (O.P.) who resigned, John Robins to be Colo, John Mapp Lieut: Colo, Rickards Dunton Major, Richard Nottingham to be Capt. in the room of John Mapp, Benjamin Dunton 1st Lieut:, Seth Powell 2nd Lieut: and John Mapp Junr. Ensign, Jonathan Stott Capt. in the room of Rickards Dunton, Thomas Evans 1st Lieut: & William Waterfield 2nd Lieut: and David Jones Ensign. 9 Sept. 1778. p. 104.

Supplied by the Vestry of Hungars Parish to sundry soldiers widows & children who died in the Continental Army.

```
Catharine Snead, the widow of Thomas Snead ................. £15.0.0
Sarah Rogers, widow of Solomon Rogers ...................... 15.0.0
Anne Heath and her children ............................... 15.0.0
Anne Brown for the support of Thos. Dillion's two children ... 15.0.0
Peter Turlington, son of Charles .......................... 13.0.0
Esme Belote's Child ....................................... 14.0.0
John Peyton's widow ........................................ 5.0.0
Holloway White's widow and children ....................... 19.0.0
Sarah Pettitt, widow of Isaiah Pettitt and two children ...... 60.0.0
William Heath's two Children ............................... 60.0.0
Elizabeth Southall, widow of Thos. Southalland child ......... 30.0.0
Catharine Moor, widow of Milburn Moor & two children ......... 40.0.0
Catharine Snead, the widow of Thomas Snead & two children .... 50.0.0
Sarah Rogers, widow of Solomon Rogers & two children ......... 50.0.0
Thomas Dillion's two children ............................. 50.0.0
Charles Turlington's child ................................ 25.0.0
Esme Belote's child ....................................... 25.0.0
Holloway White's widow & children ......................... 50.0.0
```

And the Treasury of the Commonwealth is desired to pay the same to the Churchwardens or Order. 8 Dec. 1778. p. 124.

Isaac Avery County Lieut: John Robins Colo, John Mapp Lieut: Colo, Rickards Dunton Major, Richard Nottingham Capt, Benjamin Dunton Lieut: David Jones Ensign & Jonathan Stott Capt. qualified to their several Commissions. 8 Dec 1778 - 128.

Recommended: Ezekiel McCready to be 1st Lieut: in the room of Rd: Street, Samuel Johnson 2nd lieut. in the room of Ezekiel McCready, Eyre Stockley Ensign in the room of Samuel Johnson. 8 Dec 178. p. 128.

John Stratton Junr. to be Capt. in the room of Ralph Dixon, Seth Powell to be Capt. in the room of Richard Nottingham and Wm. Waterfield to be Capt. in the room of Jonathan Stott. 14 Nov. 1780. p. 287.

John Wilkins (O.P.) to be County Lieutenant, John Mapp Colo. _____ (*no name - S.N.*) to be Lieutenant Colo. and _____ (*no name - S.N.*) to be Major.

Appointed: Hillary Stringer to be Capt. in the room of Edmund Glanvill, Thomas Nottingham, Junr. Lieut and John Haggoman Ensign. Obedience Johnson Junr. to be Capt. in the room of Shadrack Ames, John Howell Lieut: & Edmund Roberts Ensign. 9 May 1781. p. 320.

Receipts to: Thomas Nottingham from John Harmanson & William Scott, Commissioners of the Provision Law for ___ bushels of oats for the use of the Commonwealth was presented to Court & valued at the rate of 15s per bushel; to John Wilkins for 550 bushels of Indian corn, and valued at the rate of 2/6 per bushel; to Peter Warren for 36 bushels of corn valued at 2/6 per bushel.

Also a certificate of Henry Allan State quartermaster for 137 bushels oats received of Caleb Smith at York Town, valued at 18d including freight.

Also a certif: of Enock Lyon (Continental Quartermaster) for 221 bushels of oats received of Caleb Smith at York Town, valued at 18d including freight.

Also a receipt from John Wilkins Colo, John Burton Co: Lieut: to Samuel Johnson for 23 bars of Lead, fifty Cannon bolts & 1000 gun flints, for the use of the State. Allowed for the freight £5.

Also a receipt from John Seawale Commissary to James Russey assigned to William Satchell for 469d valued at 2 per pd.

Also an account of John Dowty against the Commonwealth for victualling a guard. Allowed £30.9.6, being proved & his appointment certified.

A certif: from John Smaw a Sergeant in the 1st Virginia Regiment for a boat pressed of Caleb Smith & William Cobb allowed £20. 8 May 1782. p. 231 et seq.

A claim of Isaac Johnson's against the Commonwealth for £14, also a claim of Joshua Robins for £6 which the court adjudged to be reasonable.

A claim of Peter Bowdoin for 900 bushels of corn as appears by a receipt from John Harmanson and Wm. Scott Commissioners, supplied the Commonwealth valued at 2/6 per bushel. Ordered that the same be certified as above.

A claim of John Robins for supplying a Guard with 140 lb. bread valued at 17/ pr. lb. 14 May 1782. p. 354.

A claim of Hezekiah Pitts for furnishing a Guard with 256 lbs. Bacon valued at 9d on Lamb 10/ and one peck of Salt 3/. 14 May 1782. p. 356.

Recommended: John Stratton Junr. to be Capt. in the room of Henry Wilkins who qualified.
John Darby Lieut: Colo.
William Waltham Capt. in place of Richard Nottingham who qualified.
Wm. Stott Capt. in Room of Jonathan Stott who qualified.
Hezekiah Pitts Capt. in Room of John Darby. Caleb Fisher Capt. in the room of Harrison Thomas.
John Kendall Junr. Major.
Wm. Christian Capt. in the room of Capt. Ames.
Ralph Dixon Captain who qualified.
John Mapp County Lieutenant.
Shadrack Ames Colo.
Isaac Moor Capt. in the room of John Kendall who qualified. 14 May 1782. p. 357-358.

Hezekiah Pitts capt. and Wm. White Lieutenant took the oath of fidelity to the Commonwealth and the oath of office. 15 May 1782.

A claim of John Stratton for 2444 bushels of Indian corn valued at 2/6 pr. bushel and 600 lb. of bacon valued at 10d pr. lb supplied the public in July 1780 as appears by receipt from John Harmanson & William Scott, Commissioners, ordered that the same be certified to the house of delegates. 11 June 1782. p. 361.

Hillary Stringer Capt, Francis Costin Lieut: Isaac Johnson Ensign, Obed Cary Lieut: Senior Dunton Lieut: Wm. Christian Capt, Cobb Smith, Lieut & John Bishop Ensign, took the oath of fidelity to the Commonwealth. 11 June 1782. p. 362.

Caleb Fisher Capt. took the oath of fidelity to the Commonwealth. 9 July 1782. p. 368.

A receipt from John Harmanson & Wm. Scott, Commissioners of the provision Law to John Wilkins for 600 bushels of oats allowed 16d pr. bushel. ordered &c.

Certificate of John Harmanson & William Scott, Commisrs. to Severn Nottingham for storing 422 bushels corn, allowed 2d per bushel: ordered &c.

A claim of John Harmanson, Littleton Savage & Anne Bryon £426.16.8 for sundries supplied a volunteer troop of Horse for the defense of the County, proved by the oaths of the said John Harmanson, Littleton Savage & Walter Hyslop on behalf of the said Anne Bryan -Ordered that the same be certified.

The Certificate of John Harmanson & Wm. Scott Commrs to John Robins for storing 245 bushels of corn allowed 2nd pr. bushel. Ordered &c.

The Certificate of John Harmanson & Wm. Scott Commrs to Littleton Savage for storing 350 bushels of salt at 4d & 725 bushels of Indian Corn @ 2nd - Ordered &c.

A receipt from Edward Travis to Littleton Savage for 4 bushels of Indian Meal, supplied him when on public service, allowed 2/6 pr. bushel.

Certificates of the Commrs:

to Michael Christian for storing 927 bushels of Indian Corn @ 2d. to Henry Guy for storing 1900 bushels of Indian Corn @ 2nd pr. bushel.

to Shadrack Ames for storing 600 bushels of Indian Corn @ 2d.

to John Savage Junr. for 28 lbs. Beef supplied Colo. Webb more than his part for his district @ 4d.

to John Stratton Senr for storing 60 bushels of salt @ 4d & 760 bushels of corn @ 2d.

to Geo: Brickhouse for storing 2428 bushels of corn & oats @ 2d.

The account of Thomas Spady & others amounting to £12.7.3 ordered to be Certified &c." 14 Oct. 1782 - pp. 383 et seq.

Ordered that the Commissary of the specific Tax pay to Katherine ____ pepper wid. of Milborn Moor dec'd. who died in the continental Service, for the support of herself & children as the law directs.

The claim of Isaac Moor for receiving & storing 1103 1/2 bushels of Grain of the specific tax was allowed @ 2nd pr. Bushel.

A Claim of John Bloxom for receiving & storing 948 bushels of Do also at 2nd pr. Bushel.

Elizabeth Robins account of 12/ allowed for carting the Grain of the specific tax. 14 Jan. 1783. p. 398.

ORDER BOOK 1783 - 1787.

A receipt of A. Petrie to William Simpkins for sundries supplied a detachment of men under the Command of Captain Samuel Edden and valued at 5 dollars was allowed by the Court & ordered to be certified. A receipt from the same to John Stratton for sundries supplied as above and valued at five dollars, was allowed by the Court, and ordered to be certified. 8 July 1783. p. 10.

The Court doth allow to John Wilkins late County Lieutenant his account against the Commonwealth, for sundries supplied a detachment under the command of Capt. Davenport, amounting to ninety pounds three Shillings & 24/4. 12 Aug 1783 -p., 21

Branson Dalby to be allowed £1.16.0 for three Sheep furnished a Guard in 1782 under the Command of Colo. Shadrack Aimes - also allowed 6/1 p for 24 lbs. of pork furnished a Company on Hog island under the Command of Major John Kendall. 14 Oct. 1783. p. 32.

Recommended: John Darby to be County Lieutenant, Custis Kendall Colo, John Kendall Lieutenant Colo, John Robins Major, Arthur Downing Junr. Capt. in the room of Caleb Fisher, William Scott Capt. in the room of Isaac Moor, Francis Costin Capt. in the room of John Stratton Junr. 14 Oct. 1783. p. 34.

From Colo. John Darby to Henry Guy for provisions supplied a guard under the command of Lieutenant Holt, and valued at £9.15.0. 15 Oct. 1783. p. 38.

Elizabeth Southall is the widow of Thomas Southall dec'd. a soldier in the 9th Virginia Regiment; he died in the continental Service, leaving also a child who is still living and is about nine or ten years. 11 July 1786. p. 497.

ORDER BOOK 1808-1816
On the motion of Hezekiah Pitts - Hezekiah Pitts is the eldest brother of William Pitts who died a soldier in the American Army.
Molly Scarborough is the widow of John Scarborough, dec'd.

On the motion of Revel Watson - Nancy Smaw, Sally Biggs, Christopher Biggs & Elizabeth Watson are the legal heirs & representatives of John Smaw dec'd. 11 Sept. 1809. p. 94.

Elizabeth Barecraft, Thomas Speakman, William S. Speakman, Betsey

Speakman, Amey Wingate, John Tyler, Sally Bell & Polly Tyler are the heirs of Henry Speakman who was a soldier in the American Army during the Rev. War. 9 Oct 1809. p. 105.

Eborn Heath who died a soldier in the Rev. War, was an Uncle of Seth Heath. 8 Jan 1810. p. 115.

James Johnson, Rosey Johnson, Isaac Johnson & Peggy Johnson, Sally Travis, Peggy Wise, Mary Badger, Susey Roberts and Jenney Milliner are the heirs of Edmund Davis, a soldier who died in the Rev. War. 14 Jan 1811. p. 182.

Betsey James, Sally & Christopher Kelly are the heirs of Peter Kelly a soldier who died in the continental Army. 11 Feb. 1811. p. 184.

John Scott, Nancy Hall, Shadrack, William, James & Betsey Hall, children of James Hall & Esther his wife, who was a sister of Henry Scott, are the heirs of said Henry Scott who died a soldier in the Rev. War. 8 Apr. 1811. p. 198.

Edward L. Snead of Accomack County is the son of Smith Snead dec'd. of this County & he is the same child referred to in the will of the testator as the child with which his wife was then pregnant, which will bears date the 18th day of October, 1792. 13 May 1816. p. 28.

On 9 July 1821 appeared in open Court, Meshack Waterfield aged about 60 years, resident in Northampton County, who declares he served in the Rev. War; he enlisted in a Company then commanded by Philip Sansum in the County; he was marched to & joined the Regiment in South Carolina commanded by Colo. Campbell and continued in the service of the United States for eighteen months, the term for which he was enlisted, when he was discharged in the year 1781 at Salisbury in North Carolina. He was in the battle of Guilford Courthouse, Camden, Eutaw Springs, at the siege of Ninety six and many skirmishes. His family consists of himself, aged about sixty years as aforesaid, his Wife Sally aged about forty years, tolerably healthy, and one child named James aged about five months. 9 July 1821. p. 452.

ORDER BOOK 1822-1826

On motion of George F. Wilkins ... Nathaniel Wilkins died intestate leaving no widow nor children. Catherine Wilkins, Margaret Stratton, late Wilkins, Susan Hall, late Wilkins, Ann Kendall, late Wilkins, Henry Wilkins and Robert Wilkins his brothers and sisters of the whole blood, were his heirs at law; Margaret Stratton hath died, and Mary Ann Stratton and Susan Stratton and Sarah Stratton are her children and Eliza and Susanna Wady her grandchildren, are her only heirs. Susan Hall hath also died, and John W. Hall, Robert Hall, William Hall & Elizabeth Hall are her only children and heirs. Ann Kendall hath also died, leaving three children her only heirs viz: Littleton Kendall, John W. Kendall and Elizabeth Floyd. Said John W. Kendall is dead without any child, leaving Susan his widow to whom he devised his estate. Littleton Kendall is also dead leaving Susan Ann Kendall and Thomas Littleton Kendall his only children and heirs. Elizabeth Floyd is also dead leaving Thomas K. Floyd, Samuel L. Floyd and Elizabeth Ann Floyd her only children and heirs. Henry Wilkins is also dead, leaving Margaret Harmanson and Susan Wilkins his only children. Robert Wilkins also died intestate leaving Elizabeth his widow, George F. Wilkins and Margaret Susan Wilkins his only children and heirs. 10 June 1824 -p. 125.

COURT ORDERS - 1826 - 1831.

Leah L. Wilson, widow, Margaret Parker, Thomas L. Savage, Mary B. Savage, Elizabeth U. Savage, William L. Savage, Anne, G. Lyon, wife of George A. Lyon & Susan E. Wilson, wife of Henry P.C. Wilson, are the only heirs of Thomas L. Savage dec'd., who was a brother of Nathaniel L. Savage, dec'd. 10 Mar. 1828. p. 178.

The Court appoints Severn E. Parker guardian to his daughter Margaret Parker, who is one of the heirs of Nathaniel L. Savage, dec'd. & he thereupon entered into & acknowledged a bond according to law in the penalty of $100 with Leonard B. Nottingham security thereto. 9 June 1828. p. 209.

William A. Christian & Margaret Ames, wife of Richard Ames, are the only children & heirs of William Christian dec'd. late a Lieutenant in the Virginia State Navy during the war of the revolution. 11 Oct. 1830. p. 481.

Peter Goffigon, who was a pilot in the Virginia Navy in the Rev. War left the following children, viz: Milly Goffigon, who married James Spady since dead, & Sally Goffigon who married Richard Jones & Sally his wife

& left issue Emeline Jones an infant now alive, so that Milly Spady the daughter & Emeline Jones the granddaughter are the only surviving heirs at law of the said Peter Goffigon dec'd. 14 Mar. 1831. p. 520.

Rickards Dunton, Sophia Dunton, Elizabeth Richardson & Mary Martin are the only heirs at law of Severn Dunton dec'd. a seaman in the Virginia Navy in the Rev. War. 14 Mar. 1831. p. 524.

Major Pitts appeared personally in this Court, being a Court of Record, and deposeth he is now in the 76th year of his age; in the year 1776 he enlisted as a soldier under Capt. Smith Snead in the 9th Virginia Regiment on Continental establishment, that was commanded by Colonel George Matthews; he was in the battle of Brandywine & subsequently in the engagement at Germantown & at that place he was taken prisoner of war & was confined as a prisoner of war in Philadelphia by the British. The said Major Pitts further deposeth that by reason of age & infirmity he is unable to earn a subsistence.   Following is a schedule of his property, 20 acres of arable land with some marsh attached thereto that is not worth more than $25.00 per annum, 1 horse worth about $30.00, 10 head of horned cattle worth about $40.00, Hogs worth about $12.00 -- a little household furniture worth about $25.00, one female slave aged about 76 who is chargeable. The family of the said Major Pitts consists of himself, a niece named Jemima Mears who has two children (daughters) & who owns a female slave who is the mother of four infant children. 14 Mar. 1831. p. 524.

Sophia Meers wife of Ruben Meers & Rachel Henderson, wife of John Henderson, are the only children & heirs at law of John Scott dec'd. who was the only surviving brother & heir at law of Henry Scott, a sergeant in the Virginia Militia on continental establishment during the Rev. War. 17 Mar. 1831. p. 534.

Polly Downing wife of Edmund W. P. Downing is the only daughter & heir at law of Robert Bell, a soldier in the Virginia Militia on Continental establishment in the Rev. War. 17 Mar. 1831. p. 535.

Richard Cain & William House, an infant, Mary Anne House, an infant, Barbara House, who married Thomas Hicks who is now alive & Henry House, now of legal age, are the only surviving heirs at law of William House, supposed to have been an officer in the Rev. War. Said Cain is entitled to one half of said William House's estate and William House, Mary Anne House, Barbara Hicks (formerly Barbara House) and Henry House are entitled to equal shares of the other half. 11 Apr. 1831. p. 540.

William Christian late of this County dec'd. who was a lieutenant in the Virginia State Navy during the Rev. War & whose Will was recorded in the office of this Court on the 10th day of February, 1800, left at his death the following children: William A. Christian, Margaret, the wife of Richard Ames, George E. Christian & John Christian and no other child nor the descendant of any other child; the said George E. Christian & John Christian the residuary legatees of the said William Christian are both dead unmarried intestate & without issue. 11 July 1831.

ORDER BOOK 1831-1836.

Kendall Groten, & the children of Elizabeth Garrison, who was a daughter of John Groten, are the only heirs at law of said John Groten, dec'd. a soldier in the army of the Revolution. 14 Nov. 1831. p. 16.

Margaret Harmanson & Susanna Wilkins, daughters of Henry Wilkins, who was one of the children & heirs of Nathaniel Wilkins an officer in the Army of the Revolution are both dead; Margaret Harmanson left no child or issue & Susanna Wilkins married George Mason by whom she left children unknown to this Court & the said children, or their descendants, of Susanna Mason (formerly Wilkins) by George Mason her husband (who is also dead) are the only heirs at law of Henry Wilkins dec'd. 17 Nov. 1831. p. 31.

NOTE:The above is unquestionably an error. Henry Wilkins was the brother, not the "child" of Nathaniel - See previous order certifying the heirs of Nathaniel Wilkins; also subsequent order on p. 17 this vol.

On the motion of Miers W. Fisher ... John Fisher an ensign during the Rev. War died without issue leaving two brothers his only heirs at law, to-wit: George Fisher & William Fisher - The said George & William Fisher, brothers of John, are both dead & George left the following heirs: John R., Caleb, Ann, Miers W. & Edwin J. Fisher; John R. Fisher is living, Caleb Fisher is dead leaving Margaret Susan his only heiress, Ann married David Ewing & is now his widow & Miers W. & Edwin J. Fisher are living. William Fisher died leaving Samuel P., Sally, Thomas, William & Polly his only heirs at law - Samuel P. is living; Sally married Charles

Nelson & is now his widow; Thomas is living; William Jr. is dead leaving William, son of William, Jr., Margaret Sarah & Mary his only heirs at law; Polly married Richard Nottingham & both are dead leaving William J. Nottingham the only heir at law of the said Polly.   John R. Fisher, Margaret Susan Fisher, Ann Ewing, Miers W. Fisher, Edwin J. Fisher, Sam'l P. Fisher, Sally Nelson, Thomas Fisher, William Fisher, Margaret Sarah Fisher, Mary W. Fisher & William J. Nottingham are the only heirs at law of John Fisher an ensign as aforesaid. 13 Feb. 1832. p. 53.

John Fisher an ensign during the Rev. War died intestate; George Fisher & William Fisher his two brothers died leaving wills; Caleb Fisher one of the sons & heirs of George Fisher died intestate & James Fisher (who was not mentioned in a certificate of this Court made at the last term) another son & heir of the said George Fisher died in Baltimore, leaving a will; the said William Fisher died leaving a will, & Sally Fisher his widow & one of his legatees is dead leaving a will; William Fisher the son & one of the heirs of the said William Fisher is dead leaving a will & Polly Nottingham (formerly Polly Fisher) the daughter of William the brother of John, died intestate. 15 Mar. 1832. p. 71.

Stephen Warrington, a quarter Master on board the Galley Accomack during the Rev. War died leaving the following children: Sally, now the wife of William Parsons, Margaret, now the wife of William Whitehead, John K. Warrington, Samuel Warrington, Ann S., now Ann S. Briggs, Smith L. Warrington & Thomas J. Warrington, all of whom are living except John K. Warrington who has since the death of the said Stephen Warrington died leaving the following children: Lovea, Sally & John T. Warrington, all of whom are living, and the said Sally Parsons, Margaret Whitehead, Samuel Warrington, Anne S. Briggs, Smith L. Warrington, Thomas J. Warrington, Lovea, Sally & John T. Warrington are the only heirs at law of the said Stephen Warrington dec'd. 13 Aug. 1832. p. 118.

Cassandra Mapp, wife of John C. Mapp, Michael R. Savage, Susage Wescoat, wife of Hezekiah, John Savage, George Savage, Robert Rodgers, James Rodgers, Jane Rodgers, Edward Rodgers, Robert James, Peggy Savage, Rosy Johnson, wife of Jeptha, William Addison (of Thomas) & Betsy Bunting are heirs at law of Michael James, late a Lieutenant in the Virginia State Navy. 13 Aug. 1832. p. 119.

On the motion of Vespasian Ellis, who offered affidavits to the Court tending to show that a Stephen Warrington other than the one mentioned in an order & certificate made this day, was the man who was an officer in the State Navy of Virginia, the Court, without meaning to prejudice or in any way whatsoever effect the rights of any of the parties or to decide the question between them, doth order that the said order & certificate in relation to Stephen Warrington made this date be rescinded. 13 Aug. 1832. p. 120.

> *Note: The heirs of Stephen Warrington were certified by the Accomack Court 17 Jan. 1852, and they were identical with those certified by the Northampton Court in 1832 - The heirs of John K. Warrington, son of Stephen, were certified by the Accomack Court 26 Dec. 1853 - See p. 76 of this book.*

On 13 August 1832, appeared in open Court, Isma Fletcher a resident of the county, aged nearly 80 years, declares he served in the Militia of the County of Northampton from about 17 years of age till free from duty by reason of his age. Whilst serving in the Militia aforesaid he was drafted during the Rev. War to keep guard at various places in Northampton County & to defend the County from depredations. He lived at that time on Hog Island where he was born & raised & where he has ever since resided, which Island was much exposed & was under arms a great portion of each year during the war. Col. Mapp was Colonel of the Militia of Northampton County. This deponent served under Capt. Rickards Dunton of the Militia & attended alarms & kept guard during the war more than two years. He served nearly all the war in the Militia. Richard Savage had command of the portion of the Militia that served on Hog Island a part of the time. John Upshur, Sr., John Addison, John T. Wilson & Doctor Downing & others who can testify as to this deponent's character for truth & veracity & as to their belief his services. Isma Fletcher (his mark).
Certificate of George C. Waistcoat, a clergyman, residing in the County of Northampton, & of Charles West, relative to the above declaration. 13 Aug. 1832. p. 120 Certified.

Michael James, on whose estate John Addison administered in this Court, was a native of Northampton County, Virginia, where his relations and those entitled to distribution of his estate reside. He was a Lieutenant in the Navy of Virginia in the Rev. War and served to the end of the War.

He was retired by the board of officers of Virginia in 1784. John Addison administered on the estate of the said Michael James with the approbation of the heirs entitled to distribution of the estate, for the express purpose of receiving from the State of Virginia the amount in money due in half for life for the said Michael James. John Addison appoints Thomas M. Bayly of the County of Accomack to receive money due to the estate from the United States under the Act of Congress of July 5, 1832, entitled "An Act for liquidating & paying certain claims of the State of Virginia." 10 Sept. 1832. p. 124.

On 10 Sept. 1832 appeared before the County Court, James Carter, a resident of Hungars Parish in the County of Northampton, aged 73 years, who declares he enlisted in the Army of the State of Virginia, on her own State establishment, early in the War of the Revolution, as a private in a company of 18 months men, to garrison a Fort on Kings Creek in the County of Northhampton. He enlisted first for 18 months & served out that period at the Fort on Kings Creek aforesaid. Said Fort was under the command of a Captain William Davenport, Lieutenant Caleb Sansom & _____ Robinson, who was the ensign of the company. After the enlistment of 18 months was completed, in about 6 months after his discharge from the fort, crossed the Chesapeake Bay & enlisted for the War as a private in the 2nd Virginia State Regiment of Artillery commanded by Colonel Thomas Marshall. He enlisted at the Town of Portsmouth. Other officers of the said Regiment were Lieutenant Colonel Matthews & Major Mazeret. The 2nd Virginia State Regiment was divided into three parts, one of which was stationed at York under the command of Col. Marshall, another at Hampton under the command of Major Mazaret & the third at Portsmouth under the command of Colonel Matthews. He was attached to that portion of the regiment stationed at Portsmouth & belonged to a company commanded by a Captain William Jennings, who was soon broke. After said Jennings was broke a Captain Christopher Rhoan took charge of the company. Nathaniel Price who was 1st lieut. of the same company. About eighteen months or two years before the Siege of York a part of the Regiment to which he, the said Carter, belonged, was ordered to the South. He marched to South Carolina and was engaged in a regular action which took place at Camden at which Gen. Gates was Commander in Chief. In this action Colonel Porterfield of the Virginia line was killed; after the action at Camden, Carter returned in his company still under Capt. Roane's command to Virginia, by way of Petersburg to Richmond, from Richmond said Carter went to the siege of York. In a few months after the siege of York, he was discharged by a general Order at Richmond. He lived at the time of his entering the service in the County of Northampton. In all his services were about five years; he received from the State of Virginia a Land bounty warrant for 200 acres. Sworn 10 Sept. 1832. James X. Carter (his mark). 10 Sept. 1832. p. 125.

Nathaniel Wilkins dec'd. late of the County of Northampton, Virginia, and late a Lieutenant in the Virginia Continental Line during the war of the revolution, resided in the County & died intestate, leaving no widow or child or descendant thereof. Catherine Wilkins, Margaret Stratton, late Wilkins, Susan Hall, late Wilkins, Ann Kendall, late Wilkins, Henry Wilkins & Robert Wilkins were brothers & sisters of the said Nathaniel Wilkins & his only heirs at law at the time of his death. Margaret Stratton a sister of said Nathaniel Wilkins, died intestate, & Mary Ann Stratton, Susan Gordon, wife of John D. Gordon, Sarah Stratton, Eliza Waddey & Louisiana Waddey, now of Norfolk Borough, are her only heirs at law. Susan Hall, another sister of the said Nathaniel Wilkins, died intestate, & John W. Hall, Robert Hall, Elizabeth Hall & (no name) Hall now of Norfolk Borough, if living & if dead his issue, are the only heirs at law of the said Susan Hall dec'd. Ann Kendall, another sister of the said Nathaniel Wilkins, died intestate, & Littleton Kendall & Elizabeth Floyd, formerly Kendall, were at the time of her death her only heirs at law; the said Littleton Kendal died intestate & Susan Ann Kendall & Thomas L. Kendall, wards of Temple N. Robins, are the only children & heirs at law of the said Littleton; the said Elizabeth Floyd, formerly Kendall, died intestate leaving Thomas K. Floyd, Samuel L. Floyd & Elizabeth Ann Floyd, her only heirs at law. Henry Wilkins died intestate & Juliet Mason, now of Accomack County & Anne Ward, wife of Jacob Ward, now of Somerset County, Maryland, are the only heirs at law of the said Henry Wilkins dec'd. Robert Wilkins, another brother of the said Nathaniel Wilkins, died intestate & George F. Wilkins & Margaret Susan Wilkins, ward of Elizabeth Wilkins, are his only heirs at law.

Michael R. Savage, John Savage, George Savage, Cassandra Mapp, wife of John C. Mapp, Susanna Wescoat, wife of Hezekiah P. Wescoat, William Addison, Betsey Bunting, Robert James, Rosanna Johnson, wife of Jeptha Johnson, Margaret Savage, Elizabeth Savage, Elizabeth Pouson, wife of James Poulson, Robert Rogers, Jani Rogers, James Rogers, & Edwin Rogers are heirs at law of Michael James, late a Lieutenant in the

Virginia Navy. 10 Sept. 1832. p. 129.

On 10 September 1832 appeared in open Court Major Pitts, a resident of Northampton County, aged about 78 years, who declares he enlisted in the year 1776 as a soldier under Capt. Smith Snead in the 9th Virginia Regiment on continental establishment, commanded by Col. Mathews, for the term of two years. He was appointed a Sergeant in said Company during the same year & served as such till taken prisoner at Germantown. He was in the battle of Germantown & Brandywine, & was taken prisoner at Germantown & carried to Philadelphia Goal & confined there eight months & upwards & then exchanged & soon after returned home having been absent in service & imprisonment two years & several months. He made an application for a pension in 1831 which he understood was refused in consequence of his pecuniary situation, although he thought he was poor enough to be entitled to it. He was well acquainted with Col Cropper, Col Levin Joynes, Major Poulson, Capt. Darby, Capt. Thos. Snead, Maj. Smith Snead & all the officers in the continental line from Accomack & Northampton. He was born in Northampton County & always resided there. He has always understood that he was born in 1755 from his relations & ancestors. He received a discharge from service signed by Gen. Peter Mulenburgh which he has long since lost. He is well known to Gen. Severn E. Parker, Col. Littleton Upshur, Judge A.P. Upshur & to almost all the citizens of this County. He is well acquainted with Levin Hyslop of Accomack County who was in the same Regiment & is now living in said County & who can testify as to his services. (signed) Major Pitts. Certified - 10 Sept. 1832. p. 130.

On 11 September 1832 appeared in open Court before the County Court of Northampton John Tankard (Physician), resident of the said County, aged 73 years, who declares that in 1779 when the British forces under the Command of Gen. Mathews invaded this Commonwealth in the war of the Revolution & took possession of Norfolk. The militia on both sides of James River were called into service & at that time the said Tankard was a student of Medicine in Williamsburg & he formed a company of volunteers commanded by Capt. Miles Cary, and was marched to Hampton & he was there under the Command of Col. Marshall. When the British General Matthews withdrew his forces from Norfolk & sailed for New York, the company to which the said Tankard was attached was discharged & he returned home. When the British forces in January 1781 landed at Westover on James River under the command of General

Arnold, the Traitor, & were on their March to Richmond, the said
Tankard was in the City of Richmond & he again volunteered his services
& marched under the command of Major Miles Selden to oppose the said
Arnold. When within a few miles of the enemy, intelligence was received
that he greatly outnumbered the American forces, which was ordered to
retreat. After the retreat, the said John Tankard was residing in
Richmond & was called in Service as a soldier under the command of
Lieutenant Daniel Lambert & he was ordered to Sandy Point on James
River for the purpose of aiding the Marquis La Fayette in crossing the
said river with his forces, but he did not cross at that time. The said
Tankard was then under the command of Major Turberville. Whilst at
Sandy Point the said Tankard was placed by order of the State
Government, at the solicitation of Dr. Mathew Pope, the Director General
of the Hospitals, in the medical Staff & he the said Tankard was then
appointed assistant to the said Director General. The said Tankard
further declares that when the Marquis La Fayette about May 1781
marched through Richmond on his way to the Mountainous part of the
State, he acted as surgeon to General Peter Mulehnburg's Brigade which
composed a part of La Fayette's force: Mulehnburg however shortly after
this time took command of a corps of Cavalry and Genl. Stevens of
Culpepper County, Virginia, took command of the Brigade. John Tankard
further saith that he continued to act as Surgeon to the said Brigade from
May 1781 till some time after the surrender of the British forces at
Yorktown in October, 1781, when he was discharged from service & paid
off in depreciated paper which was $1000 for $1. - The said Tankard
further declareth that he was in actual service in the war of the
revolution between nine & ten months of which he was attached to the
medical Staff as a Surgeon. John Tankard declares he was born in
Hampton, Virginia, in January, 1759. His father's property was burned
by the British when they burnt Norfolk & Suffolk. He lived in
Williamsburg, Virginia, when he first volunteered. Since the Rev. War he
has lived a little while in North Carolina, a little while in Scotland, but for
the last forty years he has lived in the said County of Northampton where
he now lives. His services were voluntary excepting the expedition under
Lieutenant Lambert when he was called into service; he never acted as
a substitute, nor was he ever drafted. 11 Sept. 1832. p. 132.

William R. Hall, an infant, is the son & only heir at law of William Hall,
dec'd. late of Norfolk Borough, which said William was one of the children
& heirs at law of Susan Hall, formerly Susan Wilkins, a sister of

Lieutenant Nathaniel Wilkins, dec'd. formerly of this County.   Said William Hall died intestate. 12 Nov. 1832. p. 142.

George F. Wilkins as guardian of William R. Hall, infant son & heir at law of William Hall, dec'd., is authorized to sell, transfer & assign any & all certificates of script to which said William R. Hall may be entitled arising from the Revolutionary services of the late Lieut. Nathaniel Wilkins, dec'd. 12 Nov. 1832. p. 143.

Meshack Waterfield, a United States pensioner, died 18 July 1832 at his residence in this County, having first made his last will and testament in writing, appointing William W. Cutler Executor who has duly proved the same in this Court. 13 Nov. 1832. p. 148.

Jesse J. Simkins, guardian of Emeline Jones, has leave to sell & assign the Land Bounty & script to which the said Emeline Jones is entitled as infant heir of Peter Goffigon who was a Pilot in the Virginia Navy in the Rev. War. 10 Dec. 1832.

Jacob Chance who served in the Virginia Continental line in the Rev. War, died intestate. He left two brothers, William & Elijah, both of whom died intestate. William left the following children & heirs: Tinney Bell, widow of Thomas, Sally Scott, widow of John, Nancy Harrison, wife of Abel, Susan Harrison, wife of James & Sophia Chance; said Sophia Chance died intestate & John Moore is the only son & heir of said Sophia Chance. Elijah Chance left six children & heirs: Nancy Harmon, wife of Abel R. Harmon, William Chance, Elijah Chance, John Chance, Thomas Chance & Margaret Chance. The aforesaid descendants of William & Elijah Chance, brothers of Jacob Chance are his only heirs at law. 10 Dec. 1832. p. 156.

John R. Fisher, guardian of Margaret Susan Fisher; Samuel P. Fisher, guardian of William J. Nottingham & Anne W. Ewing (formerly Anne Hopkins) guardian of Susan Hopkins, or their authorized attorney, have leave to sell & assign the land bounty script to which the said Margaret Susan Fisher, William J. Nottingham & Susan Hopkins are entitled as infant heirs of John Fisher dec'd. who was an Ensign in the Army of the Revolution of the Virginia Line on continental establishment. 12 Mar. 1833. p. 179

Isaac Sterling a Revolutionary Soldier died intestate & Elizabeth Rayfield, alias Rowell & Selby Meholloms are the only heirs at law of said Isaac Sterling. 12 Mar. 1833. p. 181.

Peter Griffith, a revolutionary soldier, died intestate & John Griffith Senr, Moses Griffith, Thos. Griffith, William Griffith, Major Griffith, Nathan Griffin, John Costen and Thomas Dawson are the only heirs at law of said Peter Griffith dec'd.

John Dixon dec'd., a Revolutionary soldier died intestate & Margaret Hitchens & Betsy Hitchens are the only heirs at law of said John Dixon dec'd. 13 Mar. 1833. p. 185.

Daniel Fitchett, guardian of Margaret & Betsy Hitchens, heirs of John Dixon, dec'd. is authorized to sell & assign all certificates of script which may be issued in the names of the said Margaret & Betsy Hitchens for the services of the said John Dixon, a Revolutionary soldier. 14 Mar. 1833. p. 189.

Michael James who was a Lieutenant in the Virginia State Navy in the Rev. War died intestate, leaving one child who died shortly after the death of her father, an infant intestate & without issue. Michael James left no other child or descendant or any other child. The said Michael James left at his death the following brothers & sisters who are his heirs at Law, and no other brothers or sisters or descendants of any other brother or sister: Bridget James & Susan Savage, formerly Susan James who were sisters of the whole blood to said Michael James; and five brothers and sisters of the half blood, viz: Thomas James, Robert James, Peggy Bool, Elizabeth Savage and John Ewing. Said Bridget James has lately died having devised her whole estate to John C. Mapp the younger, William W. Mapp, Alfred N. H. Mapp and Robins W. W. Mapp. Said Susan Savage has died intestate leaving as her heirs at Law her children Michael Savage, Susanna, wife of Hezekiah P. Wescott, George Savage and Ann R. Rodgers. Said Ann R. Rogers is since dead intestate leaving as her heirs at law her children Robert, James, Edward & Jane Rodgers. Said George Savage has also died intestate leaving as his heirs at Law his children John & George. The said Thomas James has died intestate leaving as his heirs at Law his children Elizabeth, the wife of James Poulson, Cassandra, the wife of John C. Mapp, Rosey, the wife of Jeptha Johnson, Robert James, Ann Jacob, Petty Savage and one grandchild

Margaret James, the wife of John S. James who is the only child of his dec'd. son William James. The said Robert James, the half brother afsd Michael James, has died intestate leaving the following heirs at law, viz: his children Thomas James & Ainsley Dennis, formerly Ainsley James, and the following grandchildren, viz: William Oague, who was the only child of his dec'd. daughter Susan Oague, formerly Susan James, also Robert D. James, Abel James, Susan Dowty, the wife of James Dowty, and on great grandchild, viz: Maria Scott, the only child of Maria Scott, dec'd: the said Robert O. James, Abel James, Susan Dowty and Maria Scott being the only children of Sally James, daughter of said Robert James & also the children of Arthur Addison, whose names are unknown to the Court, by his deceased wife, who was another child of said Robert James. The said Peggy Bool has died intestate leaving three children, viz: Wm. Addison, Elizabeth Bunting & Robert Addison, the said Robert Addison has since died intestate leaving children whose names are unknown to the Court. The said John Ewing has since died intestate leaving Victor Ewing his only child & heir at Law. The said Elizabeth Savage, the half sister of the said Michael James is now living. 13 May 1833. p. 195.

Meshack Waterfield dec'd. was at the time of his death a pensioner of the United States; he died on 18 July 1832 testate & without leaving a widow. Jacob Waterfield, Mahala Hozier, widow of John Hozier, dec'd. & George Waterfield are the only legitimate children & heirs at law of the said Meshack Waterfield, dec'd. & the said Meshack Waterfield left no other children nor the descendant of any other child. 13 May 1833. p. 196.

Elizabeth J. Addison & William Addison are the only children & heirs of Rosey Addison, dec'd. the late wife of Arthur Addison, dec'd., the said Rosey being one of the heirs at law of Michael James, dec'd. who was a Lieutenant in the Virginia State Navy in the Rev. War, & the names of the said Elizabeth J. Addison & William Addison were unknown to the Court when an order was made on 13 May last certifying the heirs of the said Michael James dec'd. 10 June 1833. p. 203.

On 12 June 1833 appeared Thomas Rippen a resident of Northampton County, aged upwards of 80 years, who declares he enlisted in the Army of the United States in the year 1775 or 1776, in the 9th Virginia Regiment in a company which he thinks was commanded by Capt. or

Lieut. Nathl. Darby in Northampton for the term of three years as a drummer. When most of the 9th Regiment was marched away he remained at the Barracks in Northampton near Eastville & on Kings Creek & never removed from the County. Guard was kept at said places for several years & he was the only Drummer at those places. During the time he served as drummer there were recruiting officers stationed at Eastville; he was the only drummer from the time he enlisted for three years at Eastville Barracks & at Kings Creek & he was on guard as drummer during all of the time from the time of his enlistment in 1775 or 1776 till the end of his term of three years. He was engaged in no battles. Said Regiment belonged to the Continental line. Certified 12 June 1833. p. 216.

John Robins, formerly a Lieutenant in the 9th Virginia Regt during the war of the Revolution, died without issue, leaving Sally Robins & Caty Robins his half sisters & only heirs at Law. The said Sally Robins married Henry Harmanson; she died intestate, leaving as her only children & heirs at law, John Harmanson & Sukey Harmanson now the wife of Hezekiah Belote. Said Caty Robins married Matthew Harmanson; said Caty died intestate, leaving Betsey her only child & heir at law. The said Betsy died unmarried & intestate leaving Matthew Harmanson & Margaret Harmanson, her half brother & half sister her only heirs at law. 9 Sept. 183 3- p. 236.

John Waterfield, a Revolutionary soldier, died without issue & unmarried, leaving two brothers, William & Richard his only heirs at law. William died leaving two children his only heirs: Nancy & John. Nancy is now the wife of Thomas S. Brickhouse & John Waterfield is dead leaving Ann Waterfield his only daughter & only heir. Richard Waterfield died leaving two children & heirs, viz: Thomas & Peggy. The said Thomas died leaving Margaret & Thomas his children & only heirs at law & the said Peggy is now the wife of George D. White. It appears to the Court that the said Nancy Brickhouse, Ann Waterfield, Margaret Waterfield, Thomas Waterfield & Peggy White are at present the only heirs at law of the said John Waterfield, a Revolutionary soldier as aforesaid. 11 Sept. 1833. p. 248.

George D. White, guardian of Margaret & Thomas Waterfield is authorized to sell, assign & transfer all certificates of land script to which his said wards may be entitled as heirs of John Waterfield, dec'd., who was a soldier in the Rev. War. 11 Nov 1833 - 257

John C. Parramore is the son & only heir at law & residuary devisee of Capt. Thomas Parramore, who served as a Captain in the 9th Virginia Regiment in the Rev. War. 9 Dec. 1833. p. 265.

John Stockly, guardian of Maria Scott, is authorized to sell, transfer & assign all land bounty script to which his said ward may be entitled from the military services of Michael James, dec'd., in the Rev. War. 10 Feb. 1834. p. 279.

Henry Speakman, a Revolutionary soldier of the Virginia line died intestate unmarried & without issue leaving two sisters, Elizabeth & Molly & one brother, John, his only heirs at law. Elizabeth is now Elizabeth Barcraft. John Speakman died intestate, leaving William Speakman, Thomas Speakman, Sally Speakman, Molly Stoyt, ____ Biggs & Susan Speakman his only heirs. Molly died intestate, leaving Benjamin Tyler, Douglass Tyler, Sally Bell, William Warren, Sally Wingate & Henry Wingate her only heirs & the aforesaid persons are the only heirs at law of said Henry Speakman.

Betsy Kellam, widow of Hutchinson Kellam, William R. Milby & Hester Ames, wife of George C. Ames, are the only heirs at law of Salathiel Milby.

William Savage, Sr., Betsy Savage & Mary Drummond are the only heirs at law of Thamar Savage, formerly Thamar Ashby.

George Haley, one of the heirs of Samuel Haley, has been absent from this Commonwealth for seven years & more, & unheard of for the same length of time.

Francis Franklin Dunlop, a Chaplain in the Virginia Line in the Rev. War died intestate without issue, leaving as his heir at law one sister, Deborah Dunlop, who married John Robinson and died intestate, leaving children Christopher F., Benjamin F., Deborah E. C., now the wife of Holland Walker, & William D., who died intestate leaving one child, John, an infant. The said Christopher F. Robinson, Benjamin F. Robinson, Deborah E. C. Walker & John Robinson are the only heirs at Law of the said Francis Franklin Dunlop. 14 Apr. 1834. p. 292.

Lorimer Chowning & Harriet Dawson are the only heirs at law of William Chowning, said to have been a surgeon's mate in the Virginia Navy in the Rev. War. 12 May 1834. p. 296.

Thomas Kellam is the only heir at law of Thomas Salisbury, a private of the Virginia line in the war of the Revolution. 11 June 1834. p. 311.

Peggy Frost, the wife of Nathaniel Frost, & James Williams are the only children & heirs at law of Edward Williams dec'd., who was a soldier in the Ninth Regiment of Virginia Militia on continental establishment in the Rev. War. 14 July 1834. p. 314.

John Kendall, one of the residuary devisees of Custis Kendall, a captain of the Virginia Line, dec'd., died leaving as his children & heirs at Law, Mary Ann Dalby (formerly Mary Ann Kendall), the wife of Benjamin I. Dalby, Henry C. Kendall & John Kendall, all of whom are of legal age. Elizabeth B. Harmanson, another of the residuary devisees of the said Custis Kendall died leaving as her heirs at law Matthew T. & Margaret Harmanson. Littleton Kendall, another of the residuary legatees of the said Custis Kendall, dec'd. died leaving as his heirs at law Elizabeth Perrier, the wife of Gabriel B. Perrier, Custis Kendall & Littleton Kendall, the two last of whom are under the age of twenty one years. Henry Kendall, another of the residuary devisees of the said Custis Kendall, dec'd., died leaving as his heirs at law John, George & Louisa Kendall, all of whom are infants under the age of twenty one years. 11 Aug. 1834. p. 322.

The guardian of John Kendall & George Kendall (orphans of Henry Kendall, dec'd.) is authorized to sell & convey any land to which they may be entitled in the State of Ohio or elsewhere on account of the revolutionary services of Custis Kendall, dec'd., a captain of the Virginia Line. 10 Sept. 1834. p. 340.

William Christian, formerly a Lieutenant in the Virginia State Navy in the Rev. War, died in the month of January 1800. Thomas Parramore, who qualified as his administrator with the will annexed is dead. Administration de bonis non with the will annexed of said William Christian was granted by this Court on the 10 day of June 1833 to William A. Christian, who is now the only surviving child of said William Christian. 12 Nov. 1834. p. 356.

The guardian of Margaret S. Wilkins, Thomas L. Kendall & Susan Ann Kendall, is authorized to sell, assign & transfer all the script to which they were or may be severally entitled to as heirs at law of Nath'l Wilkins, dec'd., late a Lieutenant in the War of the Revolution. 13 July 1834. p. 405.

William Brown, a midshipman of the State Navy in the Rev. War died intestate leaving as his only heirs at law two sons, viz: John Brown & Richard Brown. John Brown died intestate leaving as his heirs at law four children, viz: Elizabeth, wife of William C. Gibbs, Mary Ann, wife of James Burcher, John Brown & William L. Brown of legal age. Richard Brown died intestate, leaving as his heirs at law the following children: Jane, wife of James Massinburg, Elizabeth, wife of Davis Coke, Susan, Sarah, & John Brown, infants under twenty one years of age. The said Elizabeth Gibbs, Mary Ann Burcher, John Brown, William L. Brown, Jane Massenburg, Elizabeth Coke, Susan, Sarah & John Brown are the only heirs at law of the said William Brown.

Major Matthew Donnovan of the Virginia Line in the Rev. War left as his only heir at law one brother, Samuel Donnovan, who died intestate, leaving as his only heir at law one daughter, Ann Donnovan, who married John Rollins & died intestate, leaving as her only heir her son, Richard D. Rollins, so that the said Richard D. Rollins is the only heir at law of the said Matthew Donnovan. 10 Aug. 1835. p. 414.

Sarah Ann Griffith & Frances Griffith are the only children & heirs at law of William Griffith, dec'd., who was one of the heirs of Peter Griffith, dec'd., & who died intestate.

Thomas Griffith, guardian of Sarah Ann & Frances Griffith, is authorized to sell, assign & transfer all land bounty script which may issue to his said wards as heirs of Peter Griffith, dec'd. 11 Jan. 1836. p. 443.

ORDER BOOK 1837 - 1841
Solomon Becket died intestate & without issue, & William Becket, Rosa Becket & Rachel Becket are the only heirs at law of the said Solomon Becket. 13 Feb. 1837. p. 7.

Henry Wingate, one of the heirs of Henry Speakman, dec'd., is dead intestate, & Sally Wingate is his sister & only heir at law. 8 May 1837.

p. 28.

Letters of administration de bonis non are granted upon the estate of John Reynolds, dec'd., a surgeon of the State Navy of Virginia in the war of the Revolution, unto Dr. Jesse J. Simkins, to enable him to recover the half pay due the heirs of the said John Reynolds, for the settlement of the Half pay claims of the officers of the Virginia State Line & Navy. It appears that John Reynolds, Surgeon of the State Navy died in the year 1816, leaving as his only nephew & heir at law William Lanis, the said William Lanis being the only son of Elizabeth Lanis, formerly Elizabeth Reynolds, an only sister of the said John Reynolds, so that the said William Lanis is the only heir at law of the identical John Reynolds who was a Surgeon as aforesaid of the Virginia State Navy, and the administration is granted unto the said Jesse J. Simkins with the consent of William Lanis, the heir of the said John Reynolds, dec'd. 14 Aug. 1837. p. 52.

Christopher F. Robinson, one of the heirs at law of Francis Franklin Dunlop, dec'd., has died intestate, leaving as his only heirs at law the remaining individuals (or their heirs) certified in the original proof of heirship made in this Court, viz: Benjamin F. Robinson, John Robinson & the children of Deborah E. C. Walker who is also dead. 10 June 1839. p. 225.

Sally Roberts, Sukey Hamby, Edward Downes, William Downes, Margaret Elliott, Thomas Downes, Nathaniel Downes, Betsey Moore, James Collins, Joseph Warren, William Warren, Polly Warren, Thomas Warren, Sr., George Warren, William Warren, Jr., John Warren & Eliza Peck are the only heirs at law of Joshua Sprunes, dec'd., who was a musician in the Rev. War. 8 June 1840. p. 338.

Joseph Warren, William Warren, Sr., Polly Warren, Thomas Warren, George Warren, William Warren, Jr. & Eliza Peck are the only heirs of Joseph Warren, Sr., dec'd., who was a soldier in the Rev. War. 8 June, 1840. p. 34-.

ORDER BOOK 1842-1845

William Dennis was a pensioner of the United States at the rate of eight dollars per month, was a resident of this County, and died therein on the nineteenth day of August, 1841; he left no widow, but he left an only son, named William Dennis who is of lawful age. 15 Mar. 1842.

William Stott was an officer in the Virginia State Navy in the Rev. War. He is long since dead, intestate, leaving his brother Jonathan & sister Peggy Stott his only heirs at law. The said Jonathan Stott died long since, intestate, leaving five children, viz: Laban, Rosey, Betsey, Keley & Nancy his only children & heirs at law. Laban married & moved from the Eastern to the Western Shore of Virginia, but whether he left at his death any child or children does not appear. Rosey married David Topping & died before her said husband, intestate, leaving a daughter, Nancy, her only heir at law, who married with a certain Benjamin Dunton & has since died intestate, leaving four children, David, Lavinia, Rosina & George Dunton as her only heirs at law. The said Betsey Stott married James Johnson & died, but whether she left any child or children does not appear to the Court. The said Keley Stott died intestate, leaving a son, John C. W. Stott as his only heir at law. And the said Nancy Stott married John Smith & died intestate, leaving two children, George & Ann (now wife of a certain John M. Savage) as her only heir at law. 9 May 1842.

William Dennis, late a private in the Army of the Revolution, is inscribed on the Pension List Roll of the Virginia Agency at the rate of eight Dollars pr. month to commence on the 15 day of February, 1820; the said William Dennis died on or about the 19 August 1841, in this County. 10 May 1842. p. 31.

Peggy Stott (mentioned in an order of this Court made the 9th day of May last) married Jesse Hudson & died intestate leaving her children Peggy & Nancy her only heirs at law; Peggy married Teackle Roberts & died intestate leaving her children Arthur T., Rosey (now wife of Seth Williams) & Esther (now wife of John Williams) her only heirs at law; Nancy Hudson married John Ross & died intestate, leaving her children Polly, Peggy, & John her only heirs at law. The said Polly Ross married Reuben Fisher & died intestate leaving her son John Fisher her only heir at law; Peggy Ross married George T. Belote & died intestate leaving her son George her only heir at law; & John Ross has died intestate leaving his children Jesse & Margaret Ross his only heirs at law. 14 Nov. 1842. p. 114.

On motion of Leah Johnson, the widow of Obadiah Johnson, a Navy

Pensioner of the United States, it appears to this Court by satisfactory evidence that the said Obadiah Johnson died in this County on 25 February 1842. 13 Feb. 1843. p. 162.

Susannah Armistead, who was Susannah Christian, died intestate, and Anna Revell, Susan Poulson & Ellison A. Hopkins are her only heirs at law. 9 Sept. 1844. p. 457.

Betsy Stott, daughter of Laben Stott, who married James Johnson, named in an order of this Court made on the 9 May 1842, as heir at law of William Stott, who was an officer in the Virginia State Navy in the Rev. War - and James Johnson are now dead and intestate, leaving no children nor the descendants of children, and that the heirs of her brothers & sisters, Laban, Rosey, Keley & Nancy Stott named in the aforesaid order of Court are her only heirs at law. 12 Mar. 1845. p. 554.

Walter C. Gardiner, late of this County, died on or about the ___ day of March, 1817, leaving as his only heirs at law Mary Nottingham, formerly Mary Gardiner, & Angelica Gardiner, children by his first wife, and Emma Gardiner and Sally S. Gardiner, children by his wife who survived him. The said Mary Nottingham was a sister of the whole blood of the said Angelica Gardiner, and died in 1821; Luther Nottingham, of this County, is her only son & heir at law now surviving her; the said Emma Gardiner married William B. Snead, and she died in 1843, leaving the following children as her only heirs at law: William, Samuel, Victor & Emma Snead surviving her; the said Sally S. Gardiner married Shadrack T. Ames, whom she now survives. Luther Nottingham is a nephew of the whole blood of the said Angelica Gardiner; the said Sally S. Ames is a sister of the half blood of the said Angelica Gardiner, and the children of the said Emma Snead are nephews & nieces of the half blood of the said Angelica Gardiner, and the said Luther Nottingham, Sally T. Ames, & William, Samuel, Victor & Emma Snead are the only heirs at law of the said Angelica Gardiner, late of the State of Rhode Island & formerly of this County, dec'd. 14 Apr. 1845. p. 569.

ORDER BOOK 1845 - 1851

Doct. John Tankard, late of this County, died 24 Apr. 1836. 12 Nov. 1849. p. 439.

Levinia Williams, formerly Levinia Dunton, one of the heirs of William

Stott, an officer in the Virginia State Navy died intestate, leaving two children, namely James H. Williams and John B. Williams her only children and heirs at Law. George N. Dunton, one of the heirs of the said William Stott has gone to California, leaving his brother, David A. Dunton his agent and attorney to transact his business for him. 10 Mar. 1851. p. 583.

On 15 April 1851 appeared John W. Tankard, aged 39 years, who declared he is one of the children and also the executor of the last will and testament of Doctor John Tankard, deceased, late of this County, who was a surgeon in the Virginia State Line in the Rev. War; the said Doctor John Tankard removed to and settled in this County in or about the year 1788; he resided in this County of Northampton during the last 48 years of his life; he was engaged for many years of his life as a surgeon and physician in private practice in this County, and he died in the said County on 24 April 1836, having first duly made his last Will; the said Doctor John Tankard left a widow at his death named Sarah, who died in this County on 7 February 1845. Dr. John Tankard was entitled to the benefits of the Act of Congress passed June the 7, 1832, but never received the benefits thereof, nor did his widow.

The following named persons are the children and grandchildren and great grandchildren of the said Dr. John Tankard, dec'd., and his only heirs at Law: his children now living are as follows, and four in number, to-wit:

1 - John W. Tankard, his son and his only executor.
2 - Philip Barraud Tankard, his son
3 - Mary Hursley, his daughter.
4 - Susan Garrison, his daughter, & wife of James R. Garrison.

 The grandchildren of Dr. John Tankard now living are as follows, and nine in number, to-wit:

1st - Georgianna Fitzhugh (now wife of Philip Fitzhugh), only child of George L. E. Tankard, dec'd., who was a son of Dr. John Tankard, dec'd.
2nd - Joshua Wyatt
3rd - Margaret Robins, widow
4th - John Wyatt
5th - William Wyatt
6th - Maria Mathews, wife of Lewis N. Mathews
7th - Sarah Wyatt
8th - George Wyatt, children of Margaret Wyatt, dec'd. who was a

daughter of Dr. John Tankard, dec'd.

9th - Ann Ashby, only child and daughter of Hannah Lewis, dec'd., who was a daughter of Dr. John Tankard, dec'd.

The great grandchildren of Dr. John Tankard, dec'd., who are heirs, are as follows, and are three in number, to-wit:

1st - James Wyatt, 2nd Margaret Wyatt & 3rd William Wyatt, who are the only children of James Wyatt, dec'd., who was the son of Margaret Wyatt, dec'd., who was the daughter of Dr. John Tankard, dec'd. 15 Apr. 1851. pp. 594-595.

Elizabeth Stott, who married James Johnson mentioned in a former order of this Court as one of the heirs of William Stott, who was an officer in the Virginia State Navy in the Rev. War, has died intestate, leaving John C. W. Stott her only heir at law. 15 Apr. 1851. p. 598.

John Turpin, who was an officer in the Virginia State Navy in the Rev. War, died intestate, leaving John D. Turpin his only son and heir at Law, and the said John D. Turpin also died intestate, leaving John L. Turpin, Elizabeth L. Wallace and Ann W. Turpin his only children and heirs at Law. 13 May 1851. p. 608.

William Stott, who was a Lieutenant in the Virginia State Navy in the Rev. War is dead and intestate, leaving as his only heirs at law the same heirs and in the same proportion to his Military Bounty Land as was entitled to the Military Bounty Land of William Stott who was a Boatswain in the Navy in the Rev. War. 9 June 1851. p. 612.

Thomas Rippon, who in the year 1832 filed a Declaration for a Pension for his services in the Rev. War, died in the County of Northampton on 13 December 1833, leaving Margaret Downes, Mary Ann Collins, John Rippon his only surviving children and heirs at law. 9 June 1851. p. 616.

The order made in this Court on 12 March 1845 is erroneous, and that the order made in this Court on 9 June 1851 proving John C. W. Stott to be the heir at law of Elizabeth Stott is correct. 8 Sept. 1851. p. 635.

ORDER BOOK 1851-1857

John Fisher, who was an Ensign in the Rev. War (formerly mentioned in an order of this Court) died intestate leaving George Fisher and William Fisher his only heirs at law. George Fisher is dead leaving a will, and

John R. Fisher, Miers W. Fisher, Edwin T. Fisher, James Fisher and Caleb Fisher his only heirs and legatees. James Fisher has since died leaving a will by which he gave his property to Susan Hopkins, who has since died intestate, leaving her mother Ann W. Ewing her only heir at law. Caleb Fisher died intestate, leaving Margaret S. Fisher his only heir at law. William Fisher (who was entitled to one half) also died testate, leaving William R. Fisher, Polly Nottingham, Samuel P. Fisher, Sally Nelson and Thomas B. Fisher his only legatees. William R. Fisher died intestate, leaving William R. Fisher, Margaret Fisher (now wife of John T. Johnson) Mary W. Fisher (wife of Littleton L. Read) his only heirs at law. Polly Nottingham died intestate leaving William J. Nottingham (who is still living), her only heir at law. Samuel P. Fisher is dead, leaving a will by which he gave his estate to his wife, Susan B. Fisher and his sons, Charles F. M. Fisher and Samuel P. Fisher, who are his only legatees. Sally Nelson died intestate, leaving Cincinatus Brickhouse her only heir at law.   11 Nov. 1851. p. 14.

Elizabeth Savage, one of the heirs of Michael James, who was a Lieutenant in the Rev. War, died intestate leaving Caleb Savage, Elizabeth Savage, Polly Savage, Hester Janny and Robert Savage her only heirs at law. Caleb Savage is dead, leaving a widow and Caleb R. Savage, Sally Savage, Rosey Savage, Franklin Savage and Thomas Savage his only children and heirs at law. Elizabeth Savage married William Ridly and died estate, leaving William Ridly, John Ridly, Elizabeth Ridly, Roseanna Ridly, Arinthia Ridly and Louisanna Ridly her only children and heirs at law. Polly Savage married Edmund Johnson and died intestate, leaving John H. Johnson her only heir at law, and Hester Janny died intestate, leaving William Savage and Elizabeth Savage her only heirs at law. The said William Savage died intestate, leaving Leonard, Teackle, Thomas & Margaret Savage his only heirs at law. 12 Apr. 1852. p. 57.

Sally Parsons, who was the daughter of Stephen Warrington, died intestate, leaving the following five children her only heirs at law: William W. Parsons, John G. Parsons, Samuel H. Parsons, Polly L. Parsons & Elkana B. Fitchett.   11 Apr. 1853. p. 178.

William Belote, who was one of the heirs at law of William Stott, who was a Revolutionary soldier, died a minor leaving his father, George Belote his only heir at law; and the said George Belote has since died intestate leaving Henry Belote, Benjamin Belote & Peggy Belote his only children and heirs at Law. 11 Apr. 1853. p. 181.

Lucy Stratton died in the County of Northampton, on or about 12 May 1848, intestate, leaving Ann G. Parker and Sarah S. Wilson as her only surviving children and heirs at law. 8 May 1854. p. 271.

John Phillips the warrantee named in Land Warrant No. 76,527 dated on 18 February 1853 intestate, leaving as his only heirs at law Polly S. Phillips, Margaret W. Phillips and Isabella C. Phillips, who are each over the age of 21 years. 12 June 1854. p. 288.

William Stott, who was a Boatswain in the Virginia Navy in the Rev. War died in the service, and intestate without issue, leaving his brother Jonathan Stott and a sister Peggy Stott his nearest kin; his brother Jonathan inherited his real estate; Jonathan Stott died intestate, leaving five children: Laban, Rosey, Betsy, Keeley and Nancy; Laban died intestate, leaving Virginia Fisher as his only heir at law: Rosey died intestate, and David A. Dunton, Lavinia Dunton, Rosina Dunton and George Dunton are her only heirs at law; Betsy Stott died intestate and without issue; Keeley Stott died intestate leaving John C. W. Stott as his only heir at law, and Nancy Stott died intestate leaving George Smith and Ann Savage her only heirs at law. 12 June 1854. p. 292.

William S. Whitehead guardian of Edward D. Whitehead, minor child of William Whitehead, dec'd., is authorized and directed to transfer, sell and assign Land Warrant No. 2845, dated 9 July 1855, for 160 acres, and which issued in favor of the said Edward D. Whitehead. 13 Aug. 1855. p. 400.

George P. Fitchett, guardian of William S. Whitehead, John S. Whitehead and Edward D. Whitehead, children of Peggy Whitehead, who was one of the heirs of Stephen Warrington, is authorized and appointed to receive their portion of the military land due them as heirs of the Stephen Warrington. 8 Oct. 1855. p. 411.

Miers W. Fisher is guardian of Juliet A. Fisher, who is a minor, and Nath'l. Robert Carey has married Susan Fisher; the said Juliet A. and Susan are devisees of Ann W. Ewing, dec'd., who was heir at law of Susan Hopkins, dec'd., who was devisee of James Fisher, dec'd., who was one of the legatees and devisees of George Fisher, dec'd., who was one of the

heirs at law of John Fisher (formerly mentioned in an order of this Court)
who was an Ensign in the Rev. War. 10 Mar. 1856. p. 452.

INDEX

-A-
ADDISON, Arthur,
14, 102
Elizabeth, 14
Elizabeth J., 102
John, 49, 95, 96
Robert, 102
Rosey, 14, 102
Thomas, 94
William, 14, 94, 97,
102
AILWORTH, James,
6
John B., 67, 68
AIMES, Caleb, 4
Shadrack, 89
ALLEN, Edmund R.,
67
John, 67
AMES, Anathy, 17
Ann, 17
Anna, 24
Annathy, 24
Benjamin T., 66
Capt., 38, 81, 82,
83, 87
Catey, 22
Edward, 65
Edward Thomas, 51
Elizabeth, 17, 51
Emily, 27
Emily A., 51
George C., 104
Georgianna, 27, 65
Georgianna C., 51
Hester, 104
Jesse, 27, 51
John A., 27, 51
John E., 65

Julia, 51
Levin, 17
Lovey, 76
Lovey C., 78
Margaret, 22, 91, 93
Mary, 24, 66
Mary R., 17
Matilda J., 22
Nancy, 22
Norvilla, 51, 65
Richard, 22, 91, 93
Richard T., 17, 24
Sally, 22, 27, 32, 51
Sally E., 66
Sally S., 109
Sally T., 109
Sally W., 17
Samuel, 51
Samuel W., 32
Shadrack, 37, 81,
82, 86, 87, 88
Shadrack T., 22,
109
Tabitha, 22
Thomas, 17, 27
Thomas C., 22
Thomas H., 51
Virginia M., 51
Virginia Margaret,
27
Washington, 24
Washington H., 17
ANDREWS, Elcanah,
14
Elkanah, 32, 40, 78
Hetty, 14
Isaac, 32
Ishmael, 15
Ismael, 1, 2

Jacob, 32
Joice, 32
Major, 8
Robert, 14
Samuel, 14, 78
William, 7, 8, 14,
32, 42
ANNIS, James, 7
Kessey, 56
Micajah, 7
Susan, 56
ARBUCKLE, Ann, 46
George, 5
George W., 46
ARMISTEAD,
Susannah, 109
ARNOLD, Gen., 99
ARUNDEL, Dohicky,
50
ASHBY, Ann, 111
Catherine, 9
David, 9, 27, 51, 65,
78
Elizabeth, 9, 27, 51
Elizabth, 65
Ezekiel, 9, 27, 51,
65
George, 2, 9
James, 9, 27, 43, 60,
78
John, 27, 51, 65
Levi, 27, 51
Lovey, 65
Margaret, 27, 65
Mary, 27
Molly, 27
Sally, 27, 51, 65
Samuel, 9, 27, 51
Smith, 27, 51, 65

Tamar, 27
Tamor, 27
Thamar, 104
Washbourn, 65
Washburn, 27
William, 51
ATCHISON, Samuel,
　82
Thomas, 82
AVERY, Isaac, 84, 85
AYRES, Edmund B.,
　62
Francis, 7, 21
Henry, 21
Littleton, 21
Richard J., 61
Thomas, 7, 21

-B-
BADGER, Mary, 90
BAGWELL, Augus-
　tus W., 46
Catherine B., 46
Caty, 44
Charles, 4
George P., 44
Isaiah, 63
William, 63
BAILEY, John, 17
John J., 17
Laban, 17
BALL, Christopher,
　58
James, 58
John, 58
Levi, 58
Samuel, 58
Seger, 58
William, 58
BARBER, William, 82

BARCRAFT, Eliza-
　beth, 104
BARECRAFT, Eliza-
　beth, 89
BARNES, Elizabeth,
　28
James, 56, 63, 79
Parker, 4
Spencer, 63
William, 28
BARNS, Parker, 2
BARRON, Capt., 5
BAYLY, Ann D., 46
Betsy, 32, 55, 77
Elijah, 32, 53
Elizabeth W., 46
Henny, 55
Henry, 77
John, 32
Laban, 23
Margaret P., 46
Molly, 32
Nancy, 55, 79
Polly, 55, 77
Rita, 11
Robert, 32, 53, 55,
　62, 77, 79
Sacker, 46, 59
Sally C., 46
Southey, 62
Southy, 55, 63
Thomas, 1, 40, 41
Thomas H., 46, 61
Thomas M., 25, 30,
　34, 96
William P., 46
Zadock, 11, 55, 62
BAYNE, Colmore S.,
　25
John F., 25
Walter, 25

Walter D., 25
BAYNES, Elizabeth,
　66
John, 66
BEACH, Benjamin,
　46
Catherine, 9
Caty, 10
Ezekiel, 27
Frederick, 10
James, 10, 27, 50,
　52
John, 10, 27
John Mears, 43
Levi, 52
Levin, 10, 27, 50
Mary, 10
Molly, 9, 27, 52
Peggy, 10
William, 27
BEACHAM, Caty, 49
BEARS (BEARD),
　John, 26
Matthew, 26
BEASLEY, Edmund,
　12
Fanny, 12
John, 10
Smith, 12
BEASLY, Edmund,
　50
Smith, 50
BEAVANS, John, 47
Joshua, 18
Mary, 47
Peter, 47
Sally, 18
Solomon, 47
Thomas, 47
BECKET, Betty, 47
George, 47

Mary, 47
Mason, 47
Nancy, 47
Nanny, 47
Peter, 47
Rachel, 47, 106
Rebecca, 47
Rosa, 106
Rosey, 47
Solomon, 47, 106
William, 47, 106
BEGG, John, 82
BELL, Charlotte, 28
Edmund, 54
George H., 70
Hillary, 70
James, 28, 54
Nathaniel, 4, 35
Robert, 92
Sally, 90, 104
Thomas, 100
Tinney, 100
BELOTE, Amy, 3
Benjamin, 57, 112
Betsey, 54
Charles, 48, 51
Esme, 85
George, 51, 57, 108, 112
George T., 108
Henry, 112
Hezekiah, 103
James, 47
John, 27, 48, 57
Nancy, 47
Noah, 47, 59
Peggy, 108, 112
Perry, 47
Sally, 76, 78
William, 3, 48, 51, 112

BENNETT,
Covington, 21, 54
John, 77
Littleton, 21, 54
Margaret, 77
Polly, 21, 54
Roland, 21
Rowland, 54
Samuel, 21, 54
Sinah, 41
Thomas, 8, 41
William, 21, 41, 54
BENSTON,
Elizabeth, 5
George, 5
BERRY, Ann, 68
Charles, 68
John, 68
Samuel, 68
Tinney, 68
William P., 68
BIGGS, ---, 104
Christopher, 89
Sally, 89
BIRD, John, 57
Levin, 17, 23, 24, 67
BISHOP, John, 46, 87
Nancy, 28
Southey, 28
BLAIR, John, 11, 81
BLOSOM, Elizabeth, 37
BLOXOM, Agnes, 32
Anderson P., 57
Argyle, 55
Asbury, 13
Betsey, 32
Betsy, 56
Charles, 3, 6
Comfort, 3, 6

David, 32, 56
Elijah, 31, 32, 56
Elizabeth, 17, 55
Ezekiel, 7
Ezeniah, 7
Fanny, 13, 55
George, 32, 42, 55, 56
James, 55
John, 7, 88
Leah, 64
Lemuel, 37
Levi, 7
Lucretia, 13
Mary, 31
Nancy, 32
Peggy, 13
Rachel, 32, 44, 53
Richard, 55
Rosey, 32, 56
Sally, 13
Samuel, 17
Sarah, 55
Scarborough, 64
Stephen, 32, 44, 53, 56
Stewart, 6
Tabitha, 13
Thomas, 7
Walter, 13
William, 7, 32, 56
William C., 49
Woodman, 7
BOGGS, Abel, 20, 21
Elijah, 21
James, 21, 66
William C., 21
BONEWELL,
Michael, 2
BONIWELL,
Elizabeth, 62

McKeel, 62
Thomas, 62
BONNEWELL,
  Anna, 29
  Betsey, 29
  Clement, 29
  Elijah, 29
  James, 29
  Levin, 29
  Peggy, 29
  Richard, 29
  Rosa, 29
  Sarah, 29
  Southey, 29
  Thomas, 29
BONWELL, Betsey,
  29, 51
  Betsy, 52
  Elijah, 29
  Elizabeth, 29, 59
  Harriett, 29
  Heely, 51
  James, 29
  Jesse, 10
  Leah, 29
  McKeel, 21, 26, 29
  Peggy, 10, 21, 26
  Robert, 29
  Sally, 29
  Tabitha, 29
  Thomas, 29, 59
BOOL, Peggy, 101,
  102
BOOTHE, Betsey, 18
  Charles, 18, 39
BOSTON, Elijah, 19,
  44
BOWDOIN, Edward,
  55
  Elizabeth, 55
  John, 81, 82

Nancy, 55
Peter, 86
BOWEN, James, 21
  Sally, 21
BRADFORD, Abel,
  28
  Betsey, 28
  Esther, 28
  Hetty, 70
  Jane, 28
  Mary, 28
  Zephania, 28
  Zephaniah, 28
BRICKHOUSE,
  Cincinatus, 112
  George, 88
  Nancy, 103
  Thomas S., 103
BRIGGS, Ann S., 94
  Anne S., 94
BRITMAN, John, 49
BRITNOM, John, 59
BRITTINGHAM,
  Peggy, 10
BROADWATER,
  Caleb, 8
  Covington, 21, 24
  Elizabeth, 18
  James, 25
  John, 18, 24
  Rebecca, 18
  Robert, 8
  William, 18
BROWN, Anne, 85
  Betsy, 10
  Elizabeth, 106
  Jane, 106
  John, 106
  Mary Ann, 106
  P. F., 73
  Peter F., 72

Richard, 106
Sarah, 106
Susan, 106
William, 106
William L., 106
BRYAN, Anne, 88
  Augustus, 66
  Charles, 66
  John, 66
  Margaret, 66
  Martha Jane, 66
BRYON, Anne, 88
BUDD, Eliza, 48
  John, 20, 48
  Major, 48
  Margaret, 48
  McKeel, 20
  Thomas, 20
  William, 20
  Zorobabel, 20
BULL, Betsey, 29, 75
  Charles, 75
  Custis, 36, 45, 75
  Daniel, 37, 45, 69
  Elisha, 57, 60
  Eliza, 69
  Fanny, 57, 60
  George, 22
  John, 29
  Nancy, 22, 75
  Polly, 75
  Robert, 29
  Rosey, 75
  Southy, 4
  Thomas, 57, 60
  Toby, 49
BUNDICK, Edmund,
  32
  George, 4
  Jane, 28
  John, 28

Levin, 32
BUNTING, Betsey, 97
Betsy, 94
Catherine, 49
Elizabeth, 102
Esther, 2
George, 49
Holloway, 8
Jacob, 49
John, 7
Jonathan, 8
Lear (or Leah), 48
Margaret, 8, 28
Patience, 8
Peggy, 11
Rachel, 28
Richard, 7, 28
Ritchie, 2
Sacker, 8
Sally, 11, 28
Sarah, 11
Seymour, 7
Smith, 7
Solomon, 11, 28, 48, 49
Susan, 28
Thomas, 28
William, 10
William B., 45
William Black, 8, 10
BURCHER, James, 106
Mary Ann, 106
BURTON, Benjamin, 7
Garrison, 49, 71
John, 84, 86
John B., 19, 44
Joseph, 7
Sally, 49

Sally P., 44
Sarah P., 19
Thomas, 2

-C-
CAIN, Richard, 92
CAMERON, Ann G., 78
Leah, 16, 64, 78
Sarah L., 78
CAMPBELL, Arthur, 11
Colo., 90
CANNON, Elizabeth, 31
Jesse, 31, 33
Luke, 31
CAREY, Nathaniel Robert, 113
Polly, 16
Samuel S., 16
Susan, 113
CARMINE, Sinah, 41
CARPENTER, Charles, 84
CARSS, John, 8
CARTER, James, 96
James X., 97
CARY, Miles, 98
Obed, 87
CASE, Betty, 8, 18
John, 8, 18
Sabra, 18
William, 8, 18
CHAMBERS, Edmund W., 20
Hancock, 20, 29
CHANCE, Elijah, 28, 50, 100
Jacob, 28, 100
John, 28, 50, 100

Margaret, 28, 50, 100
Nancy, 28
Shadrack, 63
Sophia, 100
Thomas, 28, 50, 100
William, 28, 100
CHANDLER, Amey, 19
Bagwell, 19
Catherine, 19
Caty, 44
Edmund, 20, 30
Edward, 34, 63
Elisha, 19
Eliza, 70, 73
Elizabeth U., 19
Euphamia, 19
John, 19
Josiah, 19
Laban, 19
Leah, 20
Littleton, 19, 39, 70, 73
Margaret E., 70, 73
Mary, 19
Mary Ann, 20, 30, 63
Mitchel, 19
Nancy, 70, 73
Susan, 39, 70, 73
Tabitha, 19
Thomas, 19, 44
William, 20
CHARNICK, Henry, 12
CHARNOCK, Elizabeth, 12
John, 12
Lovey C., 78
Molly, 12

Nancy, 12
Peggy, 12
Rosey, 12
Sally, 12
William, 12
CHASE, Alsivada, 80
Brunetta, 80
Comfort, 80
Elizabeth, 80
James M., 69
Jinny, 80
Julianna L., 69
Kendal, 80
Mary, 80
Moses B., 69
Nancy, 80
Natia, 80
Polly, 80
Reginald H., 69
Robert, 40, 73, 78, 79, 80
Sally, 78, 79, 80
Sarah C., 69
Sarah J., 69
Susan, 80
Teackle, 80
Virginia M., 69
CHESHIRE, James, 8
John, 8
CHOWNING, Lorimer, 105
William, 105
CHRISTIAN, Elizabeth, 22
George, 22
George E., 93
John, 93
Michael, 81, 82, 88
Rosey, 22
Susannah, 109

Willam A., 22
William, 39, 87, 91, 93, 105
William A., 91, 93, 105
CHRISTOPHER, Delight, 49
George, 7
CHURN, Molly, 9
Peggy, 9
Sally, 57
William, 9
CLARK, George, 49
Tully, 42, 60
CLERK, George, 4
Scarbrough, 4
COARD, William, 18
COBB, Bridget, 3
Stratton, 3, 7
Susa, 7
William, 7, 86
COKE, Davis, 106
Elizabeth, 106
COLEBURN, R., 38
Ro., 35
Robert, 2
COLLINS, Edward, 26, 43
James, 32, 43, 107
John, 54
Leah, 59, 62
Mary Ann, 111
Nancy, 26
Sally, 53
Skinner, 32
Sophia, 32
Starling, 43
Stephen, 32, 43
Susan, 47
Thomas, 32
COLONA, James, 62

COLONNA, Abel B., 75
Benjamin, 39, 75
Benjamin S., 75
James, 62
John W., 75
Major D., 75
Southy, 60
Timothy, 60
COLONY, Betsy, 58
Caty, 57
Elijah, 57, 61
Elizabeth, 5
Esther, 58
George, 5, 39, 45
Henry, 57
James, 39, 44, 45, 57, 58
John, 57, 61
John W., 57
Major, 2
Nancy, 57
Polly, 39, 60, 61
Sally, 57
Sarah, 57
Sinah, 48
Southy, 57, 60
Sukey, 62
Susan, 57, 61, 62
Timothy, 57, 60
William, 44, 57, 61
Zippa, 58
CONNER, Elisha, 47
Ezekiel, 47
COPE, Thomas, 35, 36, 38
COPES, Beverly, 24, 67
Charles, 56, 63, 79
Eliza, 20
Elizabeth, 22, 79

George, 22
Henry, 79
Hetty, 24
Margaret, 14
Molly, 4
Parker, 14, 24, 67
Peter Parker, 14,
    42
Sally, 56, 79
Savage, 79
Solomon, 4, 22
Sophia, 42
Southy, 1, 2, 4
Thomas, 1, 2, 22, 43
Thomas P., 49, 67
William, 22
CORBIN, Col., 34
Covington, 1
Edward, 64, 74
Elizabeth, 56, 61,
    64, 73, 74
George, 4
James S., 26, 67, 76
Mary Jane, 26, 76
Robert, 64, 73, 74
Sally, 71
Sarah Ann, 26, 76
William, 25
CORE, Margaret, 10
William, 10
COSTEN, John, 101
COSTIN, Francis, 87,
    89
COWGILL, Sarah G.,
    22
COX, John, 75
CRIPPEN, John, 29
Narcissa, 29
Rosa, 29
William, 7
CROCKETT, Asa, 32

Caty, 32
CROPPER, Ann, 46
Capt., 45
Catherine B., 46
Col., 35, 36, 38, 98
Covington H., 46
Eliza, 46
John, 4, 5, 13, 17,
    24, 34, 37, 46, 67
John W., 46
Kendall, 18
Margaret P., 46
Nancy, 18
Sally, 17, 46
Thomas B., 46
CUSTIS, Elizabeth,
    21
Henry, 1, 2, 4
John, 2, 40, 41
Robinson, 1
Thomas, 45
William H., 21
William R., 45
CUTLER, George,
    49, 57
William W., 100

-D-
DALBY, Ann, 17
Benjamin I., 105
Brandon, 17
Branson, 89
Lemuel, 17
Mary Ann, 105
DAMERELL, Jacob,
    7
William, 7
DARBY, Betsy, 74
Capt., 98
Darmone, 74
John, 84, 87, 89

Juliet, 72
Lovey, 74
Nancy, 57
Nathaniel, 37, 103
Peggy, 74
Severn, 7
Walter W., 74
DAVENPORT, Capt.,
    89
Julia Ann, 11
Sarah, 11
Savea, 11
William, 11, 96
DAVIS, Betsy, 69
Edmund, 90
Elizabeth, 70
Henry, 69, 77
James, 41, 44, 69
John, 13
Major, 45
Noah, 69
Polly, 55
Thomas, 11
DAWSON, Harriet,
    105
Thomas, 101
DE LA FOLIE,
    Alexis, 15
DELASTATIOUS,
    Ezekiel, 52
John, 8, 48, 51, 52
Joseph, 48, 51, 52
Narcissa, 53
Peter, 48, 51, 52
Polly, 51
Sally, 50
Thomas C., 50
William, 48, 51, 52
DENNIS, Ainsley,
    102
William, 107, 108

DEVORIX, James, 18
Zilpa, 18
DICKERSON, Jesse,
  38, 73
Peter, 82, 84
DICKINSON, Peter,
  81
DICKISON, Edward,
  7
Elizabeth, 7
DILLION, Thomas,
  85
DIX, Elizabeth, 22
Henney, 22
Isaac, 6, 22
John, 2
Molly, 22
Nancy, 56
Sally, 42
William, 10, 22, 42
William C., 22
DIXON, Capt., 84
John, 101
Ralph, 81, 82, 83,
  84, 85, 87
DOD, Nancy, 47
DOE, William, 31
DOLBY, Branson, 33
Ellen G., 17
DONNOVAN, Ann,
  106
Matthew, 106
Samuel, 106
DOUGHTY, Mary, 75
DOWNES, Edward,
  107
Margaret, 111
Nathaniel, 107
Thomas, 107
William, 107
DOWNING, Anna, 55

Arthur, 89
Doctor, 95
Edmund W. P., 92
Elizabeth, 17
Francis, 8, 9
George D., 17
John, 10, 28
John W., 17, 18
Margaret D., 17
Mary, 28
Matilda, 18
Polly, 92
William, 4, 84
DOWNS, Malinda, 72
DOWTY, James, 102
John, 86
Susan, 102
DRUMMOND,
  Agnes, 59
Ann T., 9
Cary, 31
Catherine, 16
Catherine S., 9
Caty, 71
Comfort, 71
David, 16, 17
Elizabeth, 16, 17,
  31, 71
Elizabeth H., 80
Enos, 71, 75
Henry, 16
Hill, 71
James, 6, 16, 71, 75
John, 6, 41, 71, 75
John C., 71
John P., 71, 75, 80
John R., 71
John Richard, 80
Ketturah, 71
Levin, 75
Levin J., 71

Maria, 16, 17
Mary, 9, 104
Nancy, 71, 75, 80
Noah, 71
Oliver, 75
Oliver P., 71
Patience, 71
Richard, 5, 16, 17,
  71
Richard H., 9
Sally, 71, 75
Sarah A., 17
Scipio, 71, 75
Sophia, 71
Spencer, 71
Stephen, 31, 71
Tabitha, 16, 71, 75
Tabitha J., 80
Thomas, 16, 17
William, 4, 9, 16, 71
William R., 17
William S., 9, 71
William T., 16, 17
DUNCAN, Milby, 18
Sally, 18
DUNLOP, Deborah,
  104
Francis Franklin,
  104, 107
DUNTON, Benjamin,
  84, 85, 108
Capt., 83
David, 108
David A., 110, 113
Elizabeth, 16, 78
George, 108, 113
George N., 110
John, 16
Lavinia, 108, 113
Levinia, 109

Rickards, 81, 82, 85, 92, 95
Rosina, 108, 113
Senior, 87
Severn, 92
Sophia, 92
William, 16

-E-
EAST, Betsey, 29
Betsy, 29
Elizabeth, 29
James, 29
Richard, 29
Severn, 31
Southy, 31
Southy W., 31
EDDEN, Samuel, 88
EDMUNDS, Major, 5
EDWARDS, Jacob, 43, 45, 51, 72
John, 51
John B., 72
P., 72
Sally, 73
ELLIOT, George, 48
John, 48, 49
Nancy, 48
ELLIOTT, Anna, 63
Anxel, 70
Anzell Wallace, 70
Betsey, 51
Charles, 41
Elizabeth, 72
George, 51
John, 51, 84
John B., 51
John T., 63
Littleton, 49
Littleton T., 14
Margaret, 107

Nancy, 51
Peggy, 41
Rachel, 14
Teackle, 49
William, 14, 35, 49, 70
ELLIS, Vespasian, 94
EVANS, Coventon, 8
Fanny, 53
Jesse, 9
Jessee, 3
Sally, 9
Thomas, 7, 81, 82, 85
EWELL, Elizabeth, 56
George H., 74, 77
Joseph, 46
Nancy, 57
EWING, Ann, 93, 94
Ann W., 112, 113
Anne W., 100
David, 93
John, 101, 102
Victor, 102

-F-
FIELDS, John, 18, 24, 30
John D., 18, 30
William B., 18, 30
FINEY, Edward O., 71
FINNEY, John, 8
William R., 8
FISHER, Ann, 93
Bartho., 7
Caleb, 83, 84, 87, 89, 93, 94, 112
Capt., 83
Charles F. M., 112

Edwin J., 93, 94
Edwin T., 112
George, 93, 94, 111, 113
Henry W., 49
Isaac, 58
James, 22, 94, 112, 113
John, 7, 93, 94, 100, 108, 111, 114
John R., 93, 94, 100, 112
Juliet A., 113
Maddox, 39, 72
Margaret, 112
Margaret S., 112
Margaret Sarah, 94
Margaret Susan, 93, 94, 100
Mary, 94
Mary W., 94, 112
Miers W., 93, 94, 112, 113
Naomi, 5
Polly, 93, 94, 108
Reuben, 108
Sally, 93, 94
Samuel P., 93, 94, 100, 112
Susan, 113
Susan B., 112
Thomas, 5, 49, 53, 59, 82, 83, 84, 93, 94
Thomas B., 112
Tully W., 49
Virginia, 113
William, 4, 83, 93, 94, 111, 112
William R., 112

FITCHETT, Daniel, 101
  Elkana B., 112
  George P., 113
FITZGERALD, Capt., 37
  Elijah, 2
  Elisha, 35, 36, 37
  Rosey, 19
FITZHUGH, Georgianna, 110
  Philip, 110
FLEMING, Thomas, 11
FLEMMING, Thomas, 11
FLETCHER, Edward, 72
  Isma, 71, 95
  Jesse, 72
  Thomas, 13
  Tinny, 72
FLOYD, Elizabeth, 91, 97
  Elizabeth Ann, 91, 97
  Matthew, 36
  Sally, 27, 51, 65
  Samuel L., 91, 97
  Thomas, 27, 51
  Thomas K., 91, 97
  William, 81
FOREMAN, Colmore S., 25
  Elizabeth, 25
  George W., 25
  John F., 25
  Robert, 25
  Walter D., 25
  William D., 25
FOX, Mary, 65

FROST, Nathaniel, 105
  Peggy, 105
FULWELL, Dr., 82
  Samuel, 82

-G-
GALLEY, Henry, 5
GARDENER, Sally, 51
  William, 51
GARDINER, Angelica, 109
  Emma, 109
  Mary, 109
  Sally S., 109
  Walter C., 109
GARDNER, Sally, 48, 73
  William, 48
GARNER, Sophia, 29
  William, 29
GARRETT, Capt., 37
  Elijah, 43
  Elisha, 35, 36, 37
  Robert, 37
GARRISON, Abel, 50
  Elizabeth, 93
  George, 2
  James R., 110
  Margaret, 50
  Rachel, 57
  Susan, 110
GATES, Gen., 96
GIBB, Eliza, 46
  Joseph W., 46
  William, 83
GIBBS, Elizabeth, 106
  William C., 106
GIBONS, Caty, 27

  James, 27
GILCHRIST, Capt., 38, 45
GISH, Colo., 83
GLADDING, Caroline, 49
  Jesse, 8
  John, 9, 58
  John A., 49
  Polly, 57
  Sally, 49
GLANVILL, Capt., 83
  Edmund, 86
GLANVILLE, Capt., 82
  Edmund, 81, 82
GOFFIGON, Milly, 91
  Peter, 91, 92, 100
  Sally, 91
GORDON, John D., 97
  Susan, 97
GOULD, David, 60, 62
GRANT, Edward S., 80
  Tabitha, 71, 75
  Tabitha J., 80
GRAY, Levin, 7
  Lucretia, 12
  Thomas, 7
GREER, Ann T., 21, 22
GRIFFITH, Frances, 106
  John, 101
  Major, 101
  Moses, 101
  Nathan, 101

Peter, 101, 106
Sarah Ann, 106
Thomas, 101, 106
William, 101, 106
GROTEN, John, 6, 93
Kendal, 48
Kendall, 93
Margaret, 6
GUEST, Mahala, 22
Matilda, 22
Richard, 22
GUNBEY, Col., 75
GUNTER, Laban, 29
Sally, 29
GUY, Betsy, 9
Capt., 83
Elizabeth R., 19, 31
George, 9
Henry, 81, 82, 84, 88, 89

-H-
HAGGONMAN, John, 86
HALEY, George, 104
James, 20
Samuel, 104
HALL, ---, 97
Ann, 66
Ann H., 25
Ann H. P., 19, 26
Betsey, 90
Betsy, 69
Capt., 83
Daniel R., 83, 84
Daniel Raales, 83
Dixon, 66
Eliza, 42, 66
Eliza Anne, 79
Elizabeth, 91, 97

Ephraim, 59
Ephriam, 42
Erastus, 66, 79
Esther, 90
George, 5, 42
Gilbert, 42
Henry, 71
Henry H., 19, 25, 26
James, 90
John, 42, 59
John C., 42
John W., 91, 97
Louisa, 66, 77, 79
Margaret, 25, 47, 53, 66, 79
Mary, 66, 77, 79
Mary Ann, 42
Nancy, 90
Richard, 25
Robert, 91, 97
Shadrack, 90
Susan, 91, 97, 99
Thomas, 1
William, 90, 91, 99, 100
William R., 99, 100
HAMBY, Lea, 50
Sukey, 107
HAMILTON, John, 82
HAMMOND, Tyre, 37
HAMMONS, Fanny, 32, 37
Stephen, 32, 37
Tyre, 32
HARGIS, Custis, 43
George, 43
John, 43
Margarett, 43

Nancy, 43
Sally, 43
Sophia, 43
Thomas, 43
William, 43
HARMAN, Ann, 8
Betsy, 41
Comfort, 41
Ezekiel, 7
George, 41
John, 7
Leah, 41
Levin, 7
Priscilla, 8
Sarah, 41
Zerobabel, 8
HARMANSON, Betsey, 103
Elizabeth B., 105
Henry, 103
John, 81, 86, 87, 88, 103
Margaret, 91, 93, 103, 105
Matthew, 103
Matthew T., 105
Sukey, 103
HARMON, Abel K., 28
Abel R., 100
Ann, 65
Arthur, 12
Catherine, 65
Elizabeth, 65
Henry, 35
John, 35, 65, 71
Nancy, 28, 100
Rosa, 71
Sina, 71
William, 65

HARMONS,
  Stephen, 37
  Tyre, 37
HARRIS, John, 18,
  30, 52
HARRISON, Abel,
  100
  Alexander, 39
  James, 100
  John, 45, 50
  Molly, 70
  Nancy, 100
  Susan, 100
  William, 38, 45, 50,
  70
HART, Elizabeth, 58
  John, 8
HARVEY, Patience,
  19
HASTINGS, Thomas,
  46
HAYS, William, 47,
  58
HAYWARD, Ezekiel,
  52
  Margaret, 52
  Mary, 52
  Nancy, 52
  Sally, 48, 52
  Sarah, 52
  Thomas, 52
HEATH, Anne, 85
  Babel, 10
  Eborn, 90
  Edmund, 10
  James, 10
  Leah, 49
  Luke, 82, 84
  Seth, 90
  William, 85

HENDERSON,
  Brittingham, 64,
  76
  Edward, 64, 76
  James, 64, 76
  John, 19, 64, 76, 92
  Joseph, 64, 65, 76
  Martha, 19
  Milly, 76
  Nancy, 64, 65, 76
  Rachel, 92
  Sally, 65, 76
  Samuel, 17, 76
  Sarah A., 17
  Sebastian, 65, 76
  William, 64, 76
HICKMAN, Berry,
  38
  Elijah, 8
  Ezekiel, 8
  James, 17, 24
  John Berry, 68
  Kessey, 17
  Nancy, 56
  Polly, 39, 44, 45
  Samuel, 39, 44, 45
HICKS, Barbara, 93
  Thomas, 92
HIGGINS, Mary H.,
  68
HILL, Stephen, 56
HINMAN, Alfred C.,
  57, 60
  Baily, 57, 60
  Betsy, 13
  Bundick, 46, 54
  Caty, 15, 32
  Colmore C., 57, 60
  Elijah, 7
  Galen, 15, 57
  John, 13

  Lewis, 57, 60
  Littleton A., 57, 60,
  67
  Ralph, 55, 57, 60
  Sally, 59
  William, 7
HIRMON, Sally, 49
HITCHENS, Betsy,
  101
  Margaret, 101
HOGSHIRE, Agnes,
  2, 6
  Lovey, 42
  Robert, 2, 7
  Susan, 42
  William, 7
HOLCROFT, Maria,
  50
HOLLAND, Esther,
  6
  Mary, 77
  Thomas, 77
HOLMES, Elizabeth,
  9
  Thompson, 9
HOLT, Lieut., 89
HOPKINS, Anne W.,
  100
  Ellison A., 109
  Susan, 100, 112,
  113
HORNESBY, Betsy,
  17
HORNSBY, Betty, 20
  Ezekiel, 10
  James, 10
  John, 20
  Levi, 10
  Major, 20
  Susanna, 20

HOUSE, Barbara, 92, 93
Henry, 92, 93
Mary Anne, 92, 93
William, 92, 93
HOWARD, Ezekiel, 52
Margaret, 52
Mary, 52
Nancy, 52
Nehemiah, 3
Susannah, 3
Thomas, 52
HOWELL, John, 86
HOZIER, John, 102
Mahala, 102
HUCHISON, John, 7
HUDSON, Jesse, 108
Nancy, 108
Peggy, 108
Polly, 63
HURSLEY, Mary, 110
HURST, Susanna, 16
Thomas, 16
HUTCHINSON, Dorothy, 65
Edmund, 78
Elizabeth, 70, 78
John, 7
Levi, 65
Molly, 65
Richard, 65
Robert, 65
Thomas, 65
HYSLOP, James, 70, 79
John, 13
Kendall, 9
Levin, 6, 13, 70, 79, 98

Smith, 9
Susan, 13, 70, 79
Walter, 82, 88

-I-
IMRY, James, 82
INGRAM, ---, 82
James, 82
IRONMONGER, Cornelious, 2

-J-
JACKSON, Mary, 19
Stephen, 19
JACOB, Ann, 101
Sally, 9
JAMES, Abel, 102
Ainsley, 102
Betsey, 90
Bridget, 101
Cassandra, 101
Elizabeth, 101
John S., 102
Levin, 25
Margaret, 102
Margaret D., 17
Michael, 94, 95, 96, 97, 101, 102, 104, 112
Robert, 94, 97, 101, 102
Robert D., 102
Robert O., 102
Rosey, 101
Sally, 102
Susan, 101, 102
Thomas, 101, 102
William, 102
JANNY, Hester, 112
JENKINS, John, 58

JENNINGS, William, 96
JESTER, Anny, 43
Elijah, 43
Jacob, 68
James, 43
John, 43, 59
Kendal, 43
Leah, 43
JOHNSON, Betsy, 109
Charlotte, 53
Edmund, 112
Elijah C., 37
Elizabeth, 111
Eulphamy, 53
Isaac, 86, 87, 90
James, 90, 108, 109, 111
Jeptha, 94, 97, 101
John, 55
John H., 112
John T., 112
Joshua, 61
Leah, 108
Major, 6
Margaret, 112
Nancy, 54
Obadiah, 108, 109
Obedience, 81, 82, 86
Peggy, 90
Polly, 112
Rosanna, 97
Rosey, 90, 101
Rosy, 94
Samuel, 84, 85, 86
Sarah, 56
Solomon, 2
Susan, 17, 37
Tabitha, 76

JONES, Caty, 33
David, 85
Emeline, 92, 100
Henry, 7
John, 3
Phillip, 33
Rebecca, 53
Richard, 91
Sally, 91
Sarah, 3
Wealthy, 53
William, 33
JOYNES, Ann Smith, 69
Capt., 73
Charles, 48, 55
Edward, 26, 43
Edward A., 32
John, 5, 43
John G., 14, 55
Levin, 15, 37, 38, 45, 55, 69, 98
Levin T., 45
Nancy, 26
Rebecca, 26
Reuben, 2, 3, 8
Sally, 48
Thomas R., 10, 24, 45
William, 8, 26, 43
JUSTICE, Betsey, 61, 64
Betsy, 58
George, 2, 13
Margaret, 74
Richard, 4, 39, 73, 74
Rosa, 50
Rosey, 64
Samuel, 74

Teackle, 50, 64, 73, 74
William, 39, 73

-K-
KELLAM, Betsy, 104
Elizabeth, 70
Housten, 70
Houston, 35
Hutchinson, 104
Margaret, 15
Nancy, 57
Sally, 75
Spencer, 15
Thomas, 105
KELLEY, Barbara, 31
James, 56
Nancy, 57
Rachel, 56
KELLY, Christopher, 90
Daniel, 33, 49
Jacob, 7
Joseph, 1, 2
Mary, 5
Nancy, 49
Peter, 90
Richard, 33
Sally, 90
Thomas, 7
William, 5, 33
KENDALL, Ann, 91, 97
Bowdoin, 81, 82, 83, 84
Custis, 89, 105
Elizabeth, 97
George, 105
Henry, 105
Henry C., 105

John, 81, 82, 84, 87, 89, 105
John W., 91
Littleton, 91, 97, 105
Louisa, 105
Mary Ann, 105
Susan, 91
Susan Ann, 91, 97, 106
Thomas L., 97, 106
Thomas Littleton, 91
KENNAHORN, Delany, 15, 64
William, 15, 64
KESTLAR, Jacob, 9
KETSLAUGH, Jacob, 3
Patience, 3
KILLMAN, James, 80
Nancy, 69
Polly, 80
Sally, 79
KNOX, Albert, 31
Elizabeth, 31
John, 31
Oliver, 31

-L-
LA FAYETTE, Marquis, 99
LAMBERT, Daniel, 99
Lieut., 99
LAMDEN, Charlotte, 77
Robert, 77
LAND, Alexander, 53
Rosey, 53

LANDIN, Anna, 57
LANDY, Hyacinthe
  Desire, 15
  Margaret, 15
LANG, Alexander,
  25, 56
  Rosey, 56
  Sally, 25
LANIS, Elizabeth,
  107
  William, 107
LAWRENCE, John,
  57
LECATO, John, 28
  Littleton, 28
  Nathaniel, 28
  William, 28
LECATT, Augustine,
  34 .
LECATTE, Betsy, 10
  Major, 10
LEE, Andrew, 18, 19,
  23, 48
  Nancy, 18, 19, 23
  William, 41, 48
LEWIS, Ann, 68, 74
  Betsy, 74
  Bridget, 16
  Cassey, 51
  Custis, 9
  Daniel, 46
  Edward, 74
  Elizabeth, 9, 51, 74
  George, 13, 50
  Hannah, 111
  Henry Riley, 51
  Isaac, 2
  James, 29
  John, 29, 76
  Levin, 16, 23, 24, 71
  Levin D., 76

  Mahala, 51
  Milly, 72
  Nancy, 72
  Peggy, 29
  Polly, 58
  Sally, 29, 49, 51
  Sarah, 72, 76
  Spencer, 77
  Tabitha, 71, 76
  Thomas, 41, 70, 71,
  72
  Thomas D., 76
  William, 29
LILLISTON, Anne,
  21
  Asa, 11, 28
  Edmund, 21
  Elijah, 7
  Elizabeth, 11
  Hetty, 28
  James, 17
  John, 7, 17
  Kessey, 17
  Leah, 11, 28
  Margaret, 17
  Mary, 17, 24
  Nancy, 28
  Polly, 28
  Robert, 28
  Selby, 11
  Thomas, 21
  William, 11, 28
LILLISTONE,
  Thomas, 1
LING, Alexander, 25
  Rosey, 44
LINGO, Agness, 8
  Eliza, 52
  Elizabeth, 50
  Margaret, 8
  Maria, 50

  Robert R., 50, 52
  Robinson, 8
  Thomas, 8
LINTON, Lewis, 47
  Tiffany, 78
LITCHFIELD,
  Daniel, 42
  Seymour, 16
  Thomas, 16
LOGAN, Oliver, 66
LUMBER, Andrew,
  19
  James, 18, 19, 23
  Jane, 18, 19, 23, 24
  Martha, 18, 19
  Nancy, 18
  Patience, 23
  Samuel, 18, 19, 20,
  23, 24
  Thomas, 18, 19, 20,
  23, 24
  William, 18, 19, 20,
  23, 24
LURTON, Anora, 7
  John, 7
  Levin, 7
  William, 7
LYON, Anne G., 91
  Enock, 86
  George A., 91

-M-
MCALLISTER,
  Daniel, 49
MCCOLLESTER,
  Daniel, 3
  Metty, 3
MCCREADY,
  Ezekiel, 84, 85
MCGEE, Anne, 6
  Archibald, 6

MCOLLISTER,
Daniel, 49
MADDOX, Elijah, 77
Louisa, 77
Tabitha, 61
MADDUX, Tabitha,
55
MADRICK, Elisha, 8
John, 8
MADRID, Elisha, 46
MAHORN, Robinson,
57
MAPP, Alfred N. H.,
101
Capt., 81, 83, 84
Cassandra, 94, 97,
101
Col., 95
John, 82, 85, 87
John C., 94, 97, 101
Robins W. W., 101
William W., 101
MARDICK, Elisha, 5
Elizabeth, 5
MARINER, Galin, 46
James, 47
Levin, 46, 47
Nancy, 61
Paban, 61
MARSHAL, Stephen,
1
MARSHALL,
Benjamin, 33
Betsy, 44, 56
Capt., 44, 45
Charles, 1
Col., 96, 98
Elizabeth, 53, 72
Euphemia, 53
George, 1
Hester, 72

Isaac, 80
James, 72, 78
Jenifer, 15
Jenipher, 53
John, 32
John S., 53
John T., 53
Margaret, 53, 72
Maria, 56, 64, 73,
74
Mariah, 61
Michael, 33
Milly, 72
Nancy, 33
Natia, 79, 80
Patience, 71, 72, 75,
78
Rebecca, 53
Samuel, 72
Solomon, 53
Thomas, 34, 41, 44,
96
Washington, 72
William, 53, 56
William S., 53
Zachariah, 78
MARTIN, Bersheba,
24
Edward, 7
James, 7
Mary, 92
Robert, 9
MASON, Adam, 45,
70
George, 93
Henry, 21
Jane, 21
Juliet, 97
Lucy, 21
Mary, 54
Middleton, 30

Peggy, 21
Susanna, 93
Tabitha, 75
William, 21, 70
MASSENBURG,
Jane, 106
MASSEY, Elizabeth,
53
John, 56
Patty, 56
MASSINBURG,
James, 106
Jane, 106
MATHEWS,
Anthony, 8
Col., 98
Gen., 98
John, 52
Lewis N., 110
Maria, 110
MATTHEWS, Col.,
96
Esther, 12
Gen., 98
George, 12, 13, 92
Jonathan, 84
Joseph, 1
Mehala, 12
Riley, 12
Rosey, 12
MAZERET, Major, 96
MEARS, Abel, 28
Betsey, 28
David, 55
David P., 69
Edmund, 50
Edward, 60
Elisha, 4
Elizabeth, 27, 28,
51, 56, 66, 69, 71,
75, 79

Elizabeth H., 80
Frederick, 28
George, 50, 60, 69
Hilary, 36
Hillary, 69
James, 28
Jemima, 92
Jesse, 69
John, 28
John W., 80
Leah, 10
Maria, 50, 60
Mary, 28
Milly, 50, 60
Nancy, 55, 69
Peggy, 8
Polly, 27
Robert, 10, 28
Sally, 27
Sarah A., 80
Southy, 32
Teagle, 80
Thomas, 69, 80
Thorowgood, 50, 60
Tinney, 68
William, 27, 28
William B., 69
William D., 27
MEERS, Peggy, 9
Ruben, 92
Sophia, 92
MEHOLLOMS,
Selby, 101
MELSON, Amer, 16
Amey, 23
Bridget, 16, 23
Cassey, 16, 23
Henry, 16, 23
James, 16, 18, 23,
24, 39
James Milliner, 23

James Thomas, 23
Kessey, 23
Levin, 16, 23, 25, 67
Martha, 18, 19, 23
Nancy, 44, 57
Nanny, 23
Noah, 16, 23
Noah W., 23
Noah Wyatt, 23
Rachel, 23
Samuel, 16, 23
Sarah, 29
Scarborough, 18
Scarburgh, 39
Smith, 8, 29
Thomas, 16, 23
William Henry, 23
MELVIN, James W.,
31
MENDOM,
Elizabeth, 3
Robert, 3
MERRILL, Nancy, 24
METCALF, Susanna,
43
Thomas, 6
Walter, 6
METZ, Sarah Ann,
76
MIDCAP, Cassey, 49,
51
Jesse, 49, 51
MIDDLETON,
Elizabeth, 71
William, 71
MILBY, John, 22
Salathiel, 104
William R., 104
MILES, Caty, 61
Henry, 75
Nancy, 55, 61

Sally, 49
William, 46, 49, 55
MILINER, Anna
Maria, 16
Tabitha, 16
MILLECHOPS, Ann,
21
Clara, 21
James, 21
Lavinia, 21
Mary, 21
Matilda, 21
Sally, 21
MILLENER, Smith,
2
MILLER, Francis, 82
MILLICHOPS, Ann
P., 22
Clara, 22
James, 22
Lavinia, 22
Leah, 22
Mary, 22
Matilda, 22
MILLINER, Henry, 7
James, 16
Jenney, 90
John, 16
Nancy, 16
Robert, 16, 67
Samuel, 7
Smith, 16
Southy, 16
Thomas, 16
MINSON, Edward,
48, 55
Gilbert, 48
Gillett, 55
Sally, 48, 55
Samuel, 48
MISTER, Caty, 26

James, 26
MOON (MOOR),
　Levi, 7
　Stephen, 7
MOOR, Catharine, 85
　Isaac, 87, 88, 89
　Katherine ---pepper,
　　88
　Milborn, 88
　Milburn, 85
MOORE, Betsey, 107
　Catherine, 21
　John, 32, 40, 66,
　　100
　Levi, 68
　Levin, 32
　Margaret, 66
　Polly, 56
　Rachel, 32
　Stephen, 32
　Tabitha, 65, 68
　Thomas, 11, 56, 65,
　　68
　William P., 65, 69,
　　72, 75
MOORES, William
　P., 70
MULEHNBURG,
　Peter, 99
MULENBURG, Gen.,
　45
MULENBURGH,
　Peter, 98
MUNDAY, Leah, 48
　Mary, 48
MURRAY, David, 15,
　68
　John, 15, 68

-N-

NAUDAIN,
　Margaret, 22
NELSON, Charles,
　94
　Edward, 49
　Elizabeth, 49
　James, 7, 49
　John A., 49
　Margaret, 49
　Robert, 7
　Sally, 49, 93, 94,
　　112
　Susan, 49
　Thomas, 77
NICHOLSON, John,
　4
NOCK, John, 7
　Polly, 21
　Samuel, 21
　William, 7, 10
NORTHAM, Betsy,
　53
　Custis, 21
　George, 59
　Henry, 49
　Henry B., 60
　John, 49, 60
　Milcah, 60
　Miles, 46, 58
　Nancy, 21
　Susa, 59
　Susan, 49
　William, 53
NORWORTHY,
　Rachel, 65
NOTTINGHAM,
　Leonard B., 91
　Luther, 109
　Mary, 109
　Polly, 94, 112

Richard, 84, 85, 87,
　94
　Severn, 87
　Thomas, 83, 86
　William J., 94, 100,
　　112

-O-

OAGUE, Susan, 102
　William, 102
OLDHAM, George,
　73
ONIONS, Ann Maria,
　56
　Levena Jane, 56
　Selby, 8
　Susan, 56
　Westly, 56
　William, 8
ONLY, Lovey, 74
OUTTEN, Elizabeth,
　66
　Margaret, 66
　Martha Jane, 66
　Mary, 66
　Purnell G., 66
　Shadrick W., 66
OWENS, Ann, 41
　Elizabeth, 41
　Jesse, 41
　Mary, 41
　Milcah, 41
　Sally, 41
　Samuel, 41, 42

-P-

PALMER, James T.,
　77
PARADISE, Merrill,
　58

PARKER, Anderson, 57
Ann G., 113
Betsey, 20
Caleb, 6
Clement, 1, 2, 4, 52
George, 35, 36
John, 20, 21, 30, 34, 63
John F., 52
John Riley, 4
Levin, 7, 20, 30, 34, 63
Lorenzo D., 52
Margaret, 91
Nancy, 64
Peggy, 21
Peter, 20, 30, 34, 63, 64
Revell, 20
Richard, 7, 20, 30, 34, 63
Severn E., 91, 98
Thomas, 11, 12, 14, 15, 34, 37, 40, 52
William, 1, 2, 4, 38
PARKES, Betsy, 57
Edmund, 57
James, 57
John, 40, 57, 69
Peter, 57
Raymond Melvin, 56
Sarah, 57
PARKS, Ann, 69
Charles, 13
Comfort, 13
Nancy, 13, 30
Solomon, 13, 30
PARRAMORE, John C., 104

Thomas, 1, 11, 12, 104, 105
William, 1, 4, 31, 38, 39
PARSON, Capt., 83
Sally, 76
William, 76
PARSONS, Capt., 82
John G., 112
Polly L., 112
Sally, 94, 112
Samuel H., 112
Thomas, 81, 84
William, 94
William W., 112
PAYNE, Elener, 52
Jacob, 52
PEACOCK, Nancy, 47
PEARSON, Kessey, 75
PECK, Benjamin, 2
Eliza, 107
PERKINS, Joshua, 42, 52, 61
Nimrod, 33
Sally, 52, 61
PERRIER, Elizabeth, 105
Gabriel B., 105
PETRIE, A., 88
PETTIGREW, Gavin, 26, 27
John, 4, 21, 22, 26, 68
Richard, 59, 62
PETTITT, Isaiah, 85
Sarah, 85
PEYTON, John, 85
PHILBY, George, 8

PHILIPS, Elizabeth, 26
PHILLIPS, Benjamin, 7
Betsy, 57
Charles, 7
Charlotte, 63
Comfort, 69
Elijah, 7
Handy, 52
Isabella C., 113
Jacob, 3, 20, 29, 30, 52
James, 52
John, 38, 49, 69, 70, 113
Jonathan, 39, 46, 69
Levin W., 70
Margaret W., 113
Matthias, 12
Polly, 12, 52
Polly S., 113
Rachel, 49, 57
Susan, 70
William, 20, 29
PIERCE, Elizabeth, 25
Gideon, 25
PIERSON, Robert, 83
PITT, Ann, 25
John, 19, 25
Robert, 25
PITTS, Ann, 74
Hezekiah, 82, 83, 84, 86, 87, 89
Major, 92, 98
William, 89
POLK, William, 5, 35, 36, 38
POPE, Mathew, 99

PORTERFIELD,
Col., 96
POTTER, John, 7
Susa, 7
POULSON,
Elizabeth, 101
George, 1
James, 97, 101
John, 5, 34
Major, 38, 98
Robert J., 68
Susan, 109
POUSON, Elizabeth,
97
POWELL, J. J. W.,
72
Seth, 84, 85
Solomon, 26
PRESCOTT,
Patience, 6
Thomas, 6
PRICE, Nathaniel, 96

-R-
RALEIGH, William,
11
RAMSEY, Samuel, 56
RANDOLPH,
Beverly, 6
RAYFIELD,
Elizabeth, 101
Margaret, 65
READ, Ann, 56
Edmund, 34, 45, 68
John, 7
Littleton L., 112
Mary W., 112
William P., 56
REID, Solomon, 4
REVEL, Edward, 2
REVELL, Anna, 109

Catharine, 31
Catherine, 19
Edward C., 31
Elizabeth R., 31
George C., 19, 31
James, 31
James R., 19
John, 19, 31, 68
John B., 19, 31
Margaret, 19, 31
Nathaniel F., 19, 31
Sally B., 19, 31
William, 19, 31
REW, Leah, 54, 61
Rachel, 14
Southy, 32
REYNOLDS,
Elizabeth, 107
John, 107
RHOAN,
Christopher, 96
RIBINS, John, 83
RICHARDS, John, 8
Preeson, 8
Rachel, 8
William, 8
RICHARDSON,
Betsey, 50
Daniel, 65
Elizabeth, 58, 92
James, 50
Kendall, 28
Nancy, 42, 65
Polly, 65
Sally, 65
William, 28
RICHISON, Charles,
6
Daniel, 6
William, 6
Zerobabel, 6

RIDLY, Arinthia, 112
Elizabeth, 112
John, 112
Louisanna, 112
Roseanna, 112
William, 112
RIGGS, Betsey, 61
Elizabeth, 54
George, 46
George B., 46
George R., 61
William, 46, 54, 61
RILEY, Eliza, 17
Elizabeth, 17
Ellen G., 17
Emily C., 17
George, 17
Henny, 49
John, 2, 25
Nathaniel, 17
Ramond, 2
William, 2, 16, 40,
41
William M., 17
RIPPEN, Thomas,
102
RIPPON, John, 111
Thomas, 111
ROANE, Capt., 96
ROBBINS, Juliet, 65
ROBERTS, Arthur
T., 108
Edmund, 86
Esther, 108
Peggy, 108
Rosey, 108
Sally, 107
Susey, 90
Teackle, 108
ROBERTSON, John,
50

Mary D., 79
William, 79
ROBINS, Arthur, 27, 51
Caty, 103
Elizabeth, 88
George W., 72
Isaac D., 72
John, 81, 82, 84, 85, 86, 88, 89, 103
Joshua, 86
Julia, 51
Juliet, 27
Margaret, 110
Sally, 103
Temple N., 97
Thomas, 37, 72
ROBINSON, ---, 96
Benjamin F., 104, 107
Christopher F., 104, 107
Deborah E. C., 104
John, 104, 107
William D., 104
RODGER, Capt., 4
RODGERS, Ann R., 101
Edward, 94, 101
Henry, 43
James, 6, 94, 101
Jane, 94, 101
John, 49
Rachel, 21
Robert, 49, 94, 101
William W., 21
Zerobabel, 2
ROGERS, Edwin, 97
Hester, 46
Jacob, 42, 65
James, 97

Jani, 97
John, 49, 65
Major, 65
Molly, 65
Nancy, 65
Peter, 45, 46
Robert, 49, 97
Sarah, 85
Solomon, 85
Tinney, 65
ROLLINS, John, 106
Richard D., 106
ROMAS, Adam, 33
George, 33
Henry, 33
John, 33
William, 33
ROOKS, Rachel, 12
ROSS, Betsey, 62
Betsy, 47
Charlotte, 62, 66, 77
Elijah, 7, 46
Elizabeth, 25, 53, 66, 77
Ezekiel, 80
Jacob M., 20, 46
James, 46
Jesse, 108
John, 7, 108
Jolly, 77
Levin T., 80
Margaret, 62, 66, 77, 108
Mary, 62, 66
Molly, 20
Nancy, 108
Peggy, 108
Polly, 108
Ralph, 62
Robert, 62, 66

Sally, 62, 66
Susan, 46, 80
Tully Joseph, 77
William, 25, 66
William J., 62
ROWELL, Elizabeth, 101
ROWLEY, Eliza, 72
RUSSEL, Andrew, 2
Thomas, 2
RUSSELL, Andrew, 4
Catherine, 56
Caty, 61, 62
Comfort, 63, 66
Elijah, 56
Ephraim, 61
Esther, 56
George, 29, 56
James, 61
Jamima, 11
John, 56, 61
Lucretia, 56
Molly, 61
Nancy, 61
Peggy, 29
Robert, 29, 41, 45, 56, 63, 66
Samuel, 12, 30
Sarah, 29
Solomon, 11
Thomas, 56
William, 56, 61
RUSSEY, James, 86

-S-
SALISBURY, Betsey, 26
Cassey, 21, 26, 30
Caty, 26
Coleburn, 26

Elisha, 26
Eliza, 26
Elizabeth, 21
Ezekiel, 26
George, 21, 26
George C., 21
James, 26, 30
John, 26
Joshua, 21, 26
Keziah, 26
Mary, 21, 26
Moses, 21, 26, 30
Nancy, 26
Robert, 21, 26
Sally, 26
Thomas, 26, 105
William, 21, 26
SAMPSON, Salathiel, 78
Stephen, 83
SANDFORD, Thomas, 2, 38
SANSOM, Caleb, 96
Philip, 12
SANSUM, Philip, 90
SATCHELL, Esther, 57, 58
George, 57, 58, 60, 61, 62
James, 58, 61
Jane, 58, 61
Mary, 58, 61
Polly, 57, 58
Sally, 57, 58
Sippa, 57, 58
Southy, 57, 60
Sukey, 57, 58
William, 57, 58, 61, 62, 86
Zippa, 61

SAVAGE, Ann, 108, 113
Anne, 65
Betsy, 104
Caleb, 112
Caleb R., 112
Eliza., 9
Elizabeth, 65, 97, 101, 102, 112
Elizabeth U., 91
Francis, 1, 2
Franklin, 112
George, 20, 83, 94, 97, 101
Harriet, 20
John, 9, 15, 88, 94, 97, 101
John M., 108
John R., 15
Leonard, 112
Levin, 26
Littleton, 81, 88
Major, 39
Margaret, 97, 112
Mary B., 91
Michael, 101
Michael R., 94, 97
Nancy, 26
Nathaniel L., 15, 91
Nathaniel Lytt, 81
Peggy, 94
Peter, 2
Petty, 101
Polly, 112
Richard, 4, 36, 95
Robert, 27, 112
Rosey, 112
Rowland, 9
Sally, 112
Susan, 101
Tamor, 27

Teackle, 112
Thamar, 104
Thomas, 112
Thomas L., 91
William, 9, 104, 112
William L., 91
SCARBOROUGH, Americus, 34
John, 89
Molly, 89
SCARBROUGH, Americus, 39
SCARBURGH, Americus, 4
Edmund, 1
Edward, 18
Elizabeth A., 13
Maria, 68
SCHOOLFIELD, Rosa, 52
William, 52
SCOTT, Caty, 31
George, 32
Henry, 90, 92
James, 12
John, 90, 92, 100
Maria, 102, 104
Nancy, 12, 20, 55
Sacker, 7
Sally, 100
Severn, 12, 20, 55
Suckey, 12
Susy, 32
William, 86, 87, 88, 89
SEAWALE, John, 86
SELBY, Arthur, 55
Candis, 55
Jack, 55
Simpson, 1
William, 1, 2, 4

SELDEN, Miles, 99
SHAY, Daniel, 58
  Elizabeth, 47
SHELTON, James,
  66
SHIELD, James, 50
  Margaret, 50
  Samuel, 50
  Thomas, 50
SHIPHARD, Major, 9
SHIPHERD, Ann, 9
  Solomon, 9
SHREAVES, Parker,
  58
SIMKINS, Jesse J.,
  100, 107
SIMPKINS, William,
  88
SIMPSON, Betsy, 48
  Charles, 48
  Col., 37, 73
  Comfort, 48
  Elisha, 7, 43, 48
  Hancock, 7, 16, 67
  Leah, 16
  Nancy, 3
  Salathiel, 3, 64
  Selby, 2, 4
  Southy, 43, 73, 74
  Tabitha, 7
  William, 48
SINGLETON,
  Henney, 22
  Richard, 22
  William, 22
SLOCOMB, Charles,
  54
  Samuel B., 54
  Thomas, 4, 54
  Walter S., 54
  William C., 54

SLOCUMB, Thomas,
  1
SMALL, Gillett, 63
  Louisa, 63
SMAW, John, 86, 89
  Nancy, 89
SMITH, Ann, 108
  Caleb, 81, 86
  Cobb, 87
  George, 108, 113
  John, 1, 47, 108
  Nancy, 33, 76
  Ralph, 33
  Solomon, 2
  Susan, 47
SMULLINGS,
  Rachel, 32
SNEAD, Amelia, 19
  Anna, 29, 63
  Bowdoin, 35, 45, 68
  Capt., 45
  Catharine, 85
  Charles, 5, 63
  Charles S., 49
  Edward L., 90
  Emma, 109
  George, 78
  Isaac, 29
  John, 19
  John B., 67
  John W., 18, 19, 33
  Mary, 63, 68
  Robert, 18, 19, 33,
  68
  Samuel, 109
  Smith, 5, 11, 34, 90,
  92, 98
  Tabitha, 11, 18, 39
  Thomas, 11, 12, 15,
  22, 45, 85, 98
  Victor, 109

  William, 1, 18, 63,
  109
  William B., 109
SOMERS, Abram, 26
  Ezekiel, 26
  Keziah, 26
SOUTHALL,
  Elizabeth, 85, 89
  Thomas, 85, 89
SPADY, James, 91
  Milly, 92
  Thomas, 88
SPARROW, Hessey,
  10
  Jacob, 38, 70
  John, 10
  Samuel, 70
SPEAKMAN, Betsey,
  90
  Elizabeth, 104
  Henry, 90, 104, 106
  John, 104
  Molly, 104
  Sally, 104
  Susan, 104
  Thomas, 89, 104
  William, 104
  William S., 89
SPIERS, Caleb, 50,
  60
  Margaret, 49
  Matilda, 49
  Polly, 50
SPRUNES, Joshua,
  107
SPYERS, James, 38
STAKES, Henry, 20,
  30, 63
  James, 20, 30, 63
  Nancy, 63

STALLINGS, James, 50
STANT, Edward, 64, 74
James, 80
Mary, 80
Milcah, 74
Milky, 64
STARLING, Capt., 75
Isaac, 56
STATE, Henry Allan, 86
STATEN, Joseph, 2, 4
STEPHENS, Betsey, 59
Eliza, 47
Elizabeth, 47, 59
Hetty, 58
James, 47
John, 47
Lovey, 59
Mary, 27
Nancy, 47
Polly, 57, 58
Rosey, 47, 59
Sally, 47, 59
Sarey, 47
Simon, 27, 59
Stephen, 27
William, 47
STERLING, Henry, 8
Isaac, 101
Richard, 8
William, 8
STEVENS, Gen., 99
Nancy, 8
STEVENSON, Nathaniel, 82

STEWART, George, 1, 4, 26, 67, 76, 77
STITH, Drury, 81, 82
STOCKLEY, Eyre, 81, 85
STOCKLY, Ann B., 9
Ayres, 9
Charles, 9
Charles T., 9
Harriot, 9
John, 104
Nehemiah, 9
STOKELY, Elijah, 2
STONE, Samuel S., 60, 62
STOTT, Betsey, 108
Betsy, 109, 113
Elizabeth, 111
John C. W., 108, 111, 113
Jonathan, 83, 85, 87, 108, 113
Keeley, 113
Keley, 108, 109
Laban, 108, 109, 113
Laben, 109
Nancy, 108, 109, 113
Peggy, 108, 113
Rosey, 108, 109, 113
William, 87, 108, 109, 110, 111, 112, 113
STOYT, Molly, 104
STRATTON, John, 81, 84, 85, 87, 88, 89
Lucy, 113
Margaret, 91, 97

Mary Ann, 91, 97
Sarah, 91, 97
Susan, 91
STREET, Rd:, 85
Richard, 83, 84
STRINGER, Hillary, 82, 83, 86, 87
SUMMERS, Betsey, 56
Elizabeth, 74
Horsey, 74
Richard, 74

-T-
TAIT, James, 82
TANKARD, ---, 99
George L. E., 110
John, 98, 99, 109, 110, 111
John W., 110
Philip Barraud, 110
Sarah, 110
TATHAM, Nancy, 56
Stephen, 56
TAYLOR, Airs, 57
Ayres, 60
Bartholomew, 50
Benjamin, 50, 60
Betsey, 57
Bundick, 52, 65, 76
Caty, 49
Charles, 43
Daniel, 32
Eliza, 69
Elizabeth, 52
Evans, 58
George Truet, 1, 2
Giles, 50, 58, 61, 64
Henney, 65
Henny, 76
Henry, 32, 58

Hessey, 46
Ibby, 31
Jabez, 46, 52, 58, 77
James, 43, 49, 82
Jesse, 52, 58
John, 8, 37, 57
Knevit, 46
Mary, 47, 65, 76
Mary Jane, 76
Nancy, 19, 50, 58, 61, 65, 76
Peggy, 47
Polly, 43
Preson, 19
Rachel, 30
Revell, 57
Revelle, 31
Robinson, 50
Sally, 19, 76
Selby, 46
Severn, 32
Tabitha, 69
Thomas, 61
William, 11, 19, 30, 52, 65, 76
William C., 32, 47
TEACKLE, Arthur, 5, 13, 45
Caleb, 34
James J., 13
Thomas, 1
TEAGUE, Alicia, 12
Jacob, 12, 14
THOMAS, Capt., 83
Comfort, 57
Harrison, 81, 82, 83, 84, 87
John, 83, 84
Patty, 24

THORNMAN, William, 9
THORNTON, Charles, 77
James, 7, 15
John, 77
Polly, 63
William, 58, 77
William P., 63
THORRINGTON, William, 52
TIGNAH, Priscilla, 3
TIGNAL, Dennis, 10
Rachel, 10
TIGNALL, Molly, 50
TIGNER, Rachel, 50, 52
TIGNOR, Molly, 50
TINDAL, Leah, 47
TODDISON, Phillip, 5
TOPPING, Bagwell, 20
Betsey, 30
Catherine, 5
Garret, 4, 5
Major, 5, 42
Mary, 30
Nancy, 20, 108
Rosey, 108
Sally, 21, 26, 30, 42
Smith, 21, 26
Thomas, 30
William, 30
TRADER, ELizabeth, 20
Elizabeth, 23, 49, 80
Hetty, 55, 77
Jane, 79
Jinny, 80

Parker, 20, 23
Polly, 52
Raymond, 80
Valentine, 80
Whittington, 52
TRAVIS, Edward, 88
Sally, 90
TROWER, Robert, 83, 84
William, 83, 84
TUNNELL, Betsey, 54
Isaiah, 54, 56, 61, 64, 73
James, 54, 64
Joseph, 54, 56, 64
William, 54, 56, 61, 64, 73, 74
TURBERVILLE, Major, 99
TURLINGTON, Charles, 85
Elizabeth A., 69
Jacob, 6
John, 65, 69
John H., 69
Nancy, 69
Nany, 6
Nathaniel, 69
Peter, 69, 85
Rachel, 6, 43
Sally, 65
Tabitha Beach, 46
William T., 69
TURNAL, John, 2
William, 3
TURNALL, Edmund, 57
Robert, 57
Sarah, 57
Scarborough, 29

Thomas, 29
TURNER, George, 65
  Molly, 10
  Polly, 65
  Richard, 65
TURPIN, Ann W.,
  111
  John, 111
  John D., 111
  John L., 111
TWIFORD, James, 4
  John, 4
TYLER, Benjamin,
  104
  Douglass, 104
  Elizabeth, 72
  John, 90
  Polly, 90

-U-
UNDERHILL,
  Micajah, 23
  Sarah, 23
  Thomas, 20, 23, 66
  William, 14, 20, 23,
    40, 67
UNDSILL, Micajah,
  23
  Sarah, 23
  William, 23
UPSHUR, A. P., 98
  John, 95
  Littleton, 98

-V-
VERNELSON,
  Nancy, 63
VESICK, Moses, 28
  Nathaniel, 28
VESSELS, Custis, 12
  William, 3

-W-
WADDEY, Eliza, 97
  Louisiana, 97
WADY, Eliza, 91
  Susanna, 91
WAISTCOAT,
  George C., 95
WALKER, Ann T., 33
  Deborah E. C., 104,
    107
  Dorothy, 65
  Eliza, 20
  Eliza., 9
  Elizabeth, 8, 65
  Henry, 8, 30
  Henry S., 65
  Holland, 104
  James, 8, 20, 44, 65
  John, 2, 8, 20, 58,
    65
  John B., 14, 33
  John P., 30
  John S., 8, 65
  Joseph, 47
  Levin, 14, 31, 33
  Margaret, 20
  Nehemiah, 31
  Rachel, 58
  Sally, 8, 20, 65
WALLACE,
  Elizabeth L., 111
WALLOP, Susan, 72
WALSTON,
  Euphamia, 15
  Euphemia, 53
  Samuel, 15, 53
WALTERS,
  Elizabeth, 54
  Isaac, 24, 67
  James, 54

  Rachel, 54
  Sally, 24
  Spencer, 54
  Thomas, 54
WALTHAM, Betsey,
  51
  Esther, 51
  Polly, 51
  Sally, 52
  William, 52, 87
WALTON, William,
  48
WAPLES, Edward
  P., 79
  Martha W., 79
  Mary D., 79
  Sabra, 77
  Sabra P., 53, 79
  Samuel, 35, 41, 53,
    77
  Sarah T., 79
WARD, Anne, 97
  Beadwell, 48
  Catherine, 22
  Jacob, 97
WARREN, Benjamin,
  82, 84
  George, 107
  John, 107
  Joseph, 107
  Peter, 86
  Polly, 107
  Thomas, 107
  William, 104, 107
WARRINGTON, Ann
  S., 94
  Betsy, 49
  Emily S., 78
  George, 76
  James, 46
  John, 49

John K., 76, 78, 94, 95
John R., 78
John T., 78, 94
Lovea, 94
Lovey, 76
Margaret, 94
Nancy, 76
Peggy, 76
Sally, 49, 51, 76, 94
Samuel, 76, 94
Smith, 76
Smith L., 94
Stephen, 76, 78, 94, 95, 112, 113
Thomas, 76
Thomas J., 94
William A., 78
WATERFIELD, Ann, 103
Elias, 82, 83, 84
George, 102
Jacob, 102
James, 90
John, 103
Margaret, 103
Meshack, 90, 100, 102
Nancy, 103
Peggy, 103
Richard, 103
Sally, 90
Thomas, 103
William, 82, 83, 85, 103
WATERS, Betsey, 57
Isaac, 18
Patty, 18
Sally, 18
Sarah, 56
Spencer, 46

Thomas, 18, 56
WATKINSON, Cornelius, 7
James, 9, 50, 52
Levin, 7
William, 9, 50, 52
WATSON, Americus, 8
David, 8
Elizabeth, 89
Euphany, 6
James, 75
Jesse, 8
Jno., 10
Johannas, 33
Johannes, 13
Johannis, 4
John, 7
Letitia, 8
Lucretia, 13
Obed, 8
Revel, 89
Tabitha, 10, 13
William, 45, 75
Zerobabel, 1
Zerrobabel, 2
WEBB, Colo., 88
Joseph, 54
Robert, 17, 24, 25
WELBORN, Eliza, 72
Hester, 72
John D., 72
Margaret, 72
Peter, 72
Susan, 72
WELBOURN, William, 44, 72
WELBURN, William, 34
WESCOAT, Hezekiah P., 97

Susanna, 97
WESCOTT, Hezekiah P., 101
Susanna, 101
WESSELLS, Arthur F., 56
Betsy, 77
Cathereine, 56
Delight, 56
Elizabeth, 79
Ephraim, 56, 62
Isaac, 56
James, 56, 60, 62
John, 46, 56, 60, 62
Laura, 56
Mary, 56
Molly, 62
Nancy, 56, 60, 62
Noah, 56
Richard, 56
Samuel, 56
Southy, 56
Susan, 56
William, 56, 60
WEST, Abel, 2
Benjamin, 29
Catharine, 31
Charles, 95
James, 42, 60
John, 2
Jonathan, 2
Molly, 28
Peggy, 29
Solomon, 42, 60
Thomas, 28
William, 29
WESTCOAT, Hezekiah, 94
Susage, 94
WESTON, Catharine (Kittura), 31

Ketturah, 71
William, 31
WHALEY, Isaac, 8
WHALY, William, 8
WHARTON, James, 50
WHEALTON, Scarburgh, 52
WHITE, Amey, 16
Betsey, 62
Betsy T., 16
Eliza A., 62
Elizabeth, 47, 66
Elizabeth A., 16
Elizabeth Ann, 26
Erastus, 62
Fanny, 55
George D., 103
Gustavus, 26
Henry, 18
Holloway, 85
Jacob, 55
Jacobus, 18
James, 18
James H., 62, 66
Jedediah, 8
John, 18, 46, 53
Levin, 18
Lewis, 26
Littleton S., 16
Louisa Hall, 62
Lucretia, 55
Margaret, 62, 79
Margaret I., 62
Margaret J., 66
Mary, 62
Mary E., 62, 66
Nancy, 16, 23
Peggy, 103
Polly, 49
Ralph, 66

Robert, 25, 47, 53, 62, 66, 67, 77, 79
Samuel C., 62
Sophia, 71, 75
South, 1
Sydney A., 18
Thomas, 49
William, 16, 87
William S., 26
WHITEHEAD, Edward, 76
Edward D., 113
John, 76
John S., 113
Margaret, 94
Peggy, 76, 113
William, 76, 94, 113
William S., 113
WILIS, William, 42
WILKERSON, Margaret, 42
Solomon, 53
William, 53
WILKINS, Ann, 91, 97
Anna, 63
Catherine, 91, 97
Elizabeth, 91, 97
George F., 63, 90, 91, 97, 100
Henry, 83, 84, 87, 91, 93, 97
John, 81, 84, 85, 86, 87, 89
Margaret, 91, 97
Margaret S., 106
Margaret Susan, 91, 97
Mary Anne, 63
Nathaneil, 93

Nathaniel, 90, 93, 97, 100, 106
Robert, 91, 97
Susan, 91, 97, 99
Susanna, 93
WILLET, John, 57
William, 21
WILLETT, William, 42
WILLIAMS, Edward, 105
Esther, 108
James, 105
James H., 110
John, 7, 8, 108
John B., 110
Levinia, 109
Rosey, 108
Seth, 108
Sophia, 7, 8
William, 1
WILLIS, Elizabeth, 27, 78
Littleton, 27
Molly, 27
Sally, 65
WILSON, George, 7
Henry P. C., 91
John T., 95
Leah L., 91
Sarah S., 113
Susan E., 91
WIMBRO, Ebern, 57
Ezekiel, 57
Griffin, 43
Henry, 43
John, 57
Nancy, 57
WIMBROUGH, Mary, 69
Rachel, 69

Richard, 39, 69, 73
WINDOW, Henry, 7
Levin, 2
WINGATE, Amey, 90
Henry, 104, 106
Sally, 104, 106
WISE, Betsey, 29
D. P., 46
Edward, 48
Henry A., 46, 71
John, 46, 51
John C., 46
Levin, 55
Mahala, 49, 51
Margaret, 46
McKeel, 29
Peggy, 90
Sally, 46
Tully, 2
Tully R., 46
Tully Robinson, 1
William, 46
William W., 46
WRIGHT, Abel, 27
WYATT, George, 110
James, 111
John, 110
Joshua, 110
Margaret, 110, 111
Molly, 9
Patty, 9
Sarah, 110
Susanna, 9
Thomas, 9
William, 110, 111

-Y-
YOUNG, Anna, 56
Betsey, 17, 54
Cathereine, 56
Elizabeth, 54

Jonathan, 17, 54
Margaret, 56
Sally, 54
Sarah, 25
Sarah Ann, 17, 56
Thomas, 1, 2
Thorowgood, 17, 25
William, 4, 17, 54

www.ingramcontent.com/pod-product-compliance
Lightning Source LLC
Chambersburg PA
CBHW071755090426
42737CB00012B/1831